A SEARCH FOR CHRISTIAN IDENTITY

A
SEARCH
FOR
CHRISTIAN
IDENTITY

*A Reasoning Approach to Believing
and Feeling as a Christian*

OSCAR C. PLUMB

An Exposition-Testament Book

Exposition Press
New York

EXPOSITION PRESS, INC.

50 Jericho Turnpike   Jericho, New York 11753

FIRST EDITION

SBN 0-682-47475-4

To Helen

Contents

Foreword   9

Introduction   11

Part I   THE LAUNCHING   13

  I   Perspective   15
 II   A Christian Defined   22

Part II   POWER TO BECOME   33

III   The Empowering Experience   35
 IV   What Does Faith Do?   45

Part III   THE PATHS THAT LEAD TO FAITH   59

  V   Believing and Feeling   61
 VI   Ways of Believing   73
VII   Creating the Belief and Faith Self-Image   96
VIII Achieving Faith-Creating Imaginative Experience   108

Part IV   FAITH FOR TODAY   137

 IX   Establishing Our Hopes (Beliefs) for Daily Living   139
  X   Getting the Substance of Our Hopes   162

Appendix   199
Bibliography   201

Foreword

I am most grateful for this opportunity to say "Thank you" to the many people who have made this writing possible. First, I would like to thank the members of church congregations who, week after week, have encouraged me in my efforts to present what I considered was the essence of vital religion. Beyond the pulpit were the classes in "Faith and Belief," as they were called. For twenty-five years I taught one of these classes each winter and answered all questions as clearly, as honestly, and as frankly as I could. The participants' loyalty, beyond differences and along with their probing questions, served to both challenge and inspire me. These studies left no place for religious platitudes and nice-sounding phrases, but were rather an experience in confident sharing and probing for spiritual truth.

Many have read this manuscript and have given helpful criticism. They are too numerous to mention, but, as I have said to them personally, I am most grateful for their helpfulness.

To each of my personal secretaries, through the years, I wish to express my deepest thanks. I am sure they feel a deep investment in this effort.

Last, but not least, I wish to thank my family for their part in my ministry. I am so grateful to our children for their confidence and trust in their "preacher-Dad," and to my wife for her labors at the typewriter (which have been many) and especially for her ability to hear the message of this book so many times and yet give each presentation the response of one who was hearing it for the first time.

Owing to the fact that so much of this material was conceived and nurtured in a group relationship, it is to be expected that it will serve that reader best who, after a first reading, studies it as part of a group.

The purpose of the group (as is the purpose of this book) should be, not to defend any particular culture or theological position, but rather to help each participant find what he needs in order to attain greater depth in his own spiritual life.

The summary questions throughout the book should serve to sharpen group discussions.

The numbers in the Bibliography correspond to the numbers in parentheses in the book.

Some suggestions on how to form and conduct a group can be found in the Appendix.

Introduction

I am writing this introduction in the name of all of those who have attended the "Faith and Belief" classes taught by the author. I have no fear of being contradicted by any of those participants when I say it was a growth experience. Now that the insights and inspiration of those sessions are presented in printed form to the public, it is our hope that it will do as much for the readers as it did for us in the classes.

In the strict sense of the word, this book is an adventure in sharing—we are all a part of it.

As former members of his classes, we feel that the spiritual approach of this book is especially needed in our time, when so many are saying that they cannot find "meaning" in the conventional approach to the spiritual, but, rather, they want to find a way to cut away the liturgical, ecclesiastical and theological "fat" and get to the "meat" of it. This book does just that!

You may not agree with the author all the time (especially at your first reading) but you will come away with a better understanding of how *all* religions serve their devotees and how to deepen the effectiveness of your own. As you study—not just read—this book, you will find where the hands (service), the heart (feeling), and the head (reason) must all fit together into a balanced whole to make a wholesome spiritual approach to life.

In the classes we had the feeling that it was both a sharing and growing experience for all present, including the teacher. A rather common feeling of those who finished the course was expressed by a professor of the University of Illinois when he said, "It is all twenty-five years ahead of its time."

Be that as it may, it is our firm conviction that if Christianity survives with thinking people during the next twenty-five years, it will come close to the presentation here shared.

May it serve you as it has served us. We are grateful to have this book.

ROBERT A. ATKINS, M.D., F.A.C.S.

Part I

THE LAUNCHING

As you are now, how often I, too, have taken a book from a shelf or table, examined its introductory statements and contents, and asked myself, "Will this book challenge my thinking and stretch my soul? I wonder why the author wrote it? Is this book for me?"

As the author of this book, I have had you, the reader, much in mind; and I am sure that if you will read Part I, you will have these questions answered.

In these first two chapters we launch our subject and prepare our thinking for our journey together in a search for Christian identity. I have always thought that it would be a terrible experience to find that I was in the middle of the wrong ocean because I had gotten on the wrong ship. On the other hand, to discover later that one stood on shore and watched his ship steam out to sea leaving him behind would be no less harrowing. I pray that this is the right ship for you and that, when we are launched, we will find you aboard.

CHAPTER I

Perspective

OUR QUEST: *To clarify our purpose and challenge.*

Mrs. L. N. had well recovered from a radical breast operation, and then a lump appeared in the other breast. She wrote later, "It was a staggering blow. It just seemed to be more than I could face; somehow it didn't seem worth the effort." She considered herself a Christian. What real difference did that make to her in her situation? As you read this book (page 134), you will find that it made all the difference in the world.

There are few, if any, situations in life where being a Christian could not, or should not, make a great difference. The Spirit of Christ (that which enabled Jesus to be what he was) is truly needed for all men and the whole man in our day. It is needed by those with or without education, position, or power, those who are black or white, male or female, healthy or sick, beautiful or ugly, lazy or ambitious, smart or dull, rich or poor. We must never overlook the fact that hate, greed, snobbery, bitterness, fear, and deceit are destructive in all men regardless of their position on the intellectual, economic, educational, or social ladder. On the other hand, the Spirit of Christ, as expressed in brotherhood, love, sharing, faith, and confidence, makes all men more able to create the best out of what they are and have, and at the same time it constructively guides them in their effort to be more and get more of what they want. Being a Christian is not something to be done "when and if," but something to be done now.

The question is, How do we make the Christian dynamic effective in our lives at the point of our need? As we attempt to answer this question, we are confronted by many others. A few of these questions are as follows:

1. Who is a Christian anyway?
2. What is the difference between having a Christian philosophy and being a Christian?
3. How do reason and feeling fit into a dynamic Christian approach to life?
4. How does one move from head to heart knowing?
5. Where do we get religious truth? How does it differ from the manner in which we get scientific truth?
6. What is the religious experience, and can it be attained on a reasonable and predictable basis?
7. What are we doing when we worship, pray, or have faith? What is the cosmic significance of each?
8. How do we help others and ourselves to move from fear to faith?
9. How can good Christian people hold such contradicting Christian beliefs?
10. In the light of what we know about the universe and the evolution of life, what is the best explanation of natural and moral evil?

In an effort to answer these and other questions, the author is not in any way setting forth something new about religion in general or about Christianity in particular; rather he is trying to clarify the reader's understanding of how any man's religion becomes effective in experience. Charles Darwin made an observation concerning the development of life on earth. He called it "the struggle for existence and the survival of the fittest." He was not inventing a scheme but revealing it. He was simply pointing out that this is the way God in nature works; whether it fits into our past or present thinking is not important.

In this study, we seek to move through and past the nonessentials of the Christian *Way* to its very essence. It is an examined approach to the Christian religion itself, not just to church beliefs and traditions. We are not asking what Christian group is right so that we may join it, but rather, What is the dynamic force found in all Christian groups, and how can we, in a predictable manner, obtain it and use it in our pursuit of an enriched Christian life—for all men and the whole man?

We are going to see if we can find what it is that does or can make your religion tick. Most people today wear watches which they can neither make nor repair, and they probably have no interest in knowing more about either. There is nothing wrong with this attitude as long as repairmen are available, but if they are not, the watches, though of the finest mechanism, will become purely ornamental. So does a personal religion become ornamental if it is not kept in repair. There was a time when we could go to the priest or the parson and have our religion repaired if it was not ticking properly, but this is not so any more. Vital Christianity is becoming less and less institutional and more and more personal. If we are not personally prepared to keep it in repair and improve it, it will soon be a pious decoration or an obsolete, unusable relic. Nowhere is it more true than in religion that we cannot unlock the future's portal with the past's "blood-rusty keys." Christianity will not survive as a force unless its devotees are as intellectually and emotionally in step with our times as were our worthy forefathers in step with theirs.

This effort should be especially helpful to those who sense the need for rethinking their Christian approach to life and, in so doing, the urgency of bringing all Christian thinking and practice into harmony with our age of expanding knowledge. The more we know about the created, certainly the more we shall increase our understanding of the Creator.

Since we are speaking mostly to and about Christians, it becomes imperative that we come as soon as possible to our question, Who is a Christian? We must define this person about whom and to whom we are speaking. This will be the challenge of our next chapter. We shall, in fact, present boldly and confidently what we think is both a practical and an obvious definition of a Christian. But, before we do this, may we make a few negative observations concerning any effort to define a Christian?

First, a Christian cannot be defined in terms of his liturgical, cultural, or historical stance.

On the church page of a large metropolitan newspaper a prospective worshiper found himself confronted with fifty Chris-

tian denominational advertisements competing for his attention.
Let us suppose that, on a given Sunday, all the Christian wor-
shipers of this big city were to meet in one palce. Even more
imaginatively, envision Jesus stepping to the podium, looking
out over these people from fifty denominations, and saying,
"Will all the real Christians please rise?"

When all the *true* followers of Jesus were standing, it would
be immediately evident that they did not belong to any one
church or culture, but were well distributed across them all.
This, of course, is not surprising, for little objectivity is needed
to observe that no Christian group has a monopoly on quality
of persons.

Recently Mrs. Plumb and I paid a visit to the shrine at
Lourdes, France, which is created around the vision of St. Berna-
dette. As we entered the crypt under the cathedral, there to our
right was a life-size statue of St. Peter holding a large key in
his hand, such as a mayor might give to some visiting V.I.P. As
we stood there, just looking, two women came in and rubbed
their hands over the well-polished toes of the statue with an
affection that could not have been more sincere and personal
had the statue been St. Peter himself.

Being of the Protestant tradition, this seemed to be a long
way from Christianity and very close to idolatry. As I reflected
on the experience later and thought about those two dear ladies,
I wondered what they would think of my approach to the spiritual as compared to theirs. I became convinced that they would
feel quite as negative toward mine as I had felt toward theirs,
and, interestingly enough, all three of us called ourselves Christians—followers of Christ. Certainly it was not the toe rubbing
that made them Christians; and, conversely, if I am one, it is
not because I do not rub toes. Liturgy, whether much or little,
simple or dramatic, is superficial and gives us no help whatsoever in our effort to distinguish between the real and the nominal
Christian.[1] The testimony of Christian experience makes it in-
dubitably clear that one man's approach may be good without
another man's being bad, or right for one without being wrong
for the other.[2]

Our second negative observation is that we cannot define a Christian in terms of theology. The fact of the matter is that there really is no such thing as THE Christian theology. What we have is the theology of Christians. We are a multiple-theology religion. What is more, all our denominations have multiple theologies also. There is, for instance, no such thing as a Methodist or Presbyterian or Episcopalian or Roman Catholic view of God, but rather the views of God held by the *members* of these denominations. Bishop Warburton is quoted by Joseph Priestley as saying, "Orthodox, my lord, is my doxy. Heterodoxy is another man's doxy."

Jesus lived in a time when men wrote and read "books." He was well-read in his religious tradition, yet he never wrote *any* theology. Certainly if the right theology had been so important to an effective religion (as many have tried to make it appear to be throughout the centuries) Jesus would have written some of it. His omitting to do so says something, and we will not all agree on just what it is.[3] In all honesty, we will have to agree with Paul Tillich when he says, "The attempt to give a foundation to Christian faith and theology through historical research is a failure."

When we make claims to having a Biblical theology, it is so easy to overlook the fact that equally able and devoted minds come out of the Bible with entirely different Biblical theology. At the close of a lecture at a conference of ministers in which I freely referred to the Bible in support of my thesis, a thinking young minister came to the rostrum and said accusingly, "You select the passages that support what you believe and leave the others out, don't you?" With as great a candor, I replied, "You are right, I do; All I want you to do is to confess that you and all the rest of our Christian colleagues do exactly the same thing."[4]

Harold Bosley, pastor of Christ Church Methodist in New York City, tells of his three year old son who, while playing on the beach, brought a small pail of water to him and said, "Here's the ocean, Daddy."

"That attitude," says Doctor Bosley, "is understandable in

a three year old boy, but not so much in a thirty year old who comes with a set of ideas and says, 'Here is the truth.' You may want to say to him, 'That may be the ocean, brother, but there is a lot more where that came from, and it's not in your bucket.' " One can, in fact, be a very good Christian with much or little truth in his theological bucket,[5] or the theology a Christian has in his bucket may serve more to undermine rather than to create Christ-mindedness.[6] Tracey K. Jones, Jr., from his experience in world missions, has done some thinking along this line that goes beyond Christian boundaries. He says, "Christians have as much right as anyone else to witness to their faith, but they should remember with shame the arrogance so often manifest in their past relationship with other religions.[7] Nothing is uglier than spiritual pride and the will to power cloaked in self-righteousness. To deduce that all who do not agree with Christians are damned is, in my judgment, a perversion of Christian love." Doctor Jones reinforces his observations by quoting from Nicolas Berdyaev, who says, "People managed to deduce from Christianity the most disgusting morality that has ever been known—the morality of transcendental heavenly egoism. 'The good' are so anxious to get into the Kingdom of Heaven that, in the crush at the entrance to it, they are ready to trample on a great number of their neighbors and push them down to hell—to eternal damnation. . . . This is the worst defeat that Christianity has suffered in human hearts."[8]

Later, consideration will be given to the importance of theology in Christian living; but for now, the point being made is that no particular theology can be considered essential to a practical and workable definition of a Christian.

Santayana noted this theological conflict between, and within, religious groups. He concluded that religions were nearing their end, but that he could not see how this would be any great catastrophe, as nothing lasts forever.

As over against this pessimism, Dr. Arnold Toynbee, well-known English historian and philosopher, ventures a suggestion that in 4000 A.D. the center of society will not be war, economics, or politics, but religion. He might well be right; for if meaning and the way to obtain it are not the ultimate center of living, what could be? By that time, society will certainly have its creature comforts well satiated. If Christianity is to play its rightful role in this religion of the future, then its followers must be clear-minded enough to distinguish between the wheat and the chaff—the important and the unimportant in it. From the above it should be clear that our definition must be created around that which is vital to effective Christianity in particular and to all religions in general. THIS is our venture—let us get started.

NOTES

1. Have you ever gone to a church of another denomination for worship and found that their ritual, or lack of it, got in your way? If so, why?

2. If your worship approach can be right for you but not for me, then what makes a worship service right? Should a worship service seek to be historically or psychologically sound? What is the difference?

3. Why do you think Jesus never wrote any theology?

4. Do you think there is anything wrong with our using scripture selectively?

5. Give an example of those whom you feel are good Christians with little theological truth in their bucket.

6. Give an example of how the wrong concept of God has destroyed Christian-mindedness.

7. How should a Christian relate himself to other religions, according to Jones?

8. What is Berdyaev's point here? Do you agree with him?

CHAPTER II

A Christian Defined

OUR QUEST: *To find that definition of a Christian which will account for the success and failure of all Christians, without in any way deprecating the effectiveness of our own personal approach to spiritual truth and experience.*

One can hardly expect to get all that there is to being a Christian into a definition; but he can expect to capture enough of the Christian essence to give him a sense of direction—a kind of compass that will keep him on the course though he may be uncertain about the path. It has been wisely said that if one keeps moving in the right direction, he need not have the right path. The path only adds to, or subtracts from, the ease of the journey.

Since there are sincere and effective Christians in all churches and with differing creeds, it is clear that a trustworthy definition of a Christian will have to emphasize not so much *what* Christians *believe*, but what they *do* and *feel*. The definition will have to be *experience-* and not *creed*-centered. Here is an attempt at that definition:

A Christian is one who relates in Jesus' way to God, self, others, and conditions (things and circumstances) about him.

Non-Christians may choose to say that a religious person relates in a mature way (establishing his own standard of maturity) to God, self, others, and conditions.[1]

Let us examine this definition with great care.

The Importance of Relating

The greatest thing in the world is to become the best possible person.[2] One does not do this in cloistered isolation, but in relationships with others. More than good ingredients are necessary to guarantee a good cake. The amount, the time, and the way each ingredient is added to the batter determine the final quality. A good grinding stone does not of itself produce a sharp knife; sharpness is determined by the length of time and the angle at which the blade is held against the stone. The potential fire in the match may be used to warm a house or to burn it down.

It is relatedness that counts.

In like manner, it is not the facts of God, self, others, and conditions about us that are determinative, but the way in which we relate to them. One may be weak in one or all of these relationships—weak in that he "cannot function as he was meant to function, consuming his energies in a destructive struggle rather than being freed for creative, positive experiences." (1)

Doctor Menninger says, ". . . the purpose of the analysis is to enable the individual to deal 'better' (that is, more maturely) with his internal and external problems." (2) Concerning the patient who gets well, he wrote: "Most of his expectations were never realized. Instead he only learned that one shouldn't expect to get certain things and then cry one's eyes out in disappointment or scratch out other peoples' eyes in rage." The patient needed to learn that he was *not* sick because of what had happened to him, but because of the way he had related to his experiences. (3)

An examination of our own lives will make it equally clear that we are what we are, *not* because of what we have or whom we are with (including God), but rather because of how we relate to them.[3]

A Christian Relates in Jesus' Way

If I were Buddhist, I would relate as did Buddha. If I were a Jew, I would relate as did the prophets. If I were a Muslim, I would relate as did Mohammed. But being a Christian, I will relate as did Jesus; he is, for me "The Way."

"A Christian," says Elton Trueblood, author of *The Company of the Committed,* "is a person who confesses that, amidst the

manifold and confusing voices heard in the world, there is one
Voice which supremely wins his full assent, uniting all his pow-
ers, intellectual and emotional, into a single pattern of self-giving.
That Voice is Jesus Christ. A Christian not only believes *that*
He was; he believes *in Him* with all his heart and strength and
mind." (4)

A certain counterfeiter felt that his arrest was a reflection
on his craftsmanship, and to defend it he placed before the
agent the ten-dollar bill from which the copy had been made.
To the counterfeiter's astonishment the agent said, "There is no
difference . . . and that's the trouble . . . you copied your counterfeit from a counterfeit." (5)

We are all well aware of the many interpretations of Jesus
that bombard us the moment we proclaim him as "The Way."
It will not be easy for us to avoid the counterfeit; but however
we may differ in details, we are alike in that we see in Jesus
what man is meant to be in all his relationships.[4]

We are reminded of Goethe's maxim: "If we take people as
they are, we make them worse. If we treat them as if they were
what they ought to be, we help them to become what they are
capable of becoming." (6)

It is this urge and tug that Jesus gives to all our lives when
we see that to be a Christian is to relate in his way.

Relating to God

There is no question but that man has many drives, including
ambition and sex; but he is also driven by an overriding need
for God. (7) No matter how great our skepticism, there are
occasions when, like H. G. Wells, we feel a relationship to something beyond ourselves and ask with the psalmist, ". . . whither
shall I flee from thy presence?" (Psalms 139:7 R.S.V.) God was
at the very center of Jesus' way of life.

One day some followers asked Jesus to assist in settling an
estate, making sure that everybody got his share. Jesus pointed
out that their greatest concern should be if they were ". . . rich
toward God." (Luke 12:21 R.S.V.) Jesus was "primarily inter-

ested in restoring man's relationship with the supra-human world," says Robert Leslie, "and in doing so clarified man's unique place in his own human environment." (8)

My late missionary friend and seminary classmate, Chris Jenson, was detained by the Communists in North Korea for several years. Though he suffered much privation as a prisoner and wanted very much to have his freedom again, yet at times he feared that freedom, for he was sure that he would never be as close to God with freedom as he was when in prison. (9) There is an endless number of accounts of those who were close to God during a crisis, and it was a real closeness. The unique thing about Jesus, as Chris would surely agree, was his closeness to God at all times. God was a part of his daily living, whether at a wedding reception or on the cross.

A distant tree is within the area of our awareness—we know that it is a tree. As we come closer, we see that it is an apple tree. When we arrive, we may eat an apple, sit under the tree, or climb it. The Christian is one who adds depth to his spiritual awareness. We simply cannot find in life what Jesus found unless we relate to God with Jesus' depth.[5]

Relating to Self

The Chinese symbol for "I" is crossed swords; and, we may add, all too often the swords are crossed within. Whereas the Buddhist yearns for absolute nonbeing, the Christian wants to be a better being. Where they would escape selfhood, we would master it. For Christians, there is nothing greater in the universe than selfhood.

The difference between a self-aware being and just being, is the difference between me and my pencil. My pencil is here even as I am here, but my pencil does not know it. It exists without self-awareness. *I know* that I am here. We Christians think of Jesus as the highest expression of selfhood that has ever lived on our earth.

Samuel Johnson once said: "My chief vocation in life is to escape from myself." He was making an emphasis, but not stating a fact; for the end of life is to find ourselves, even as Jesus found himself. This is the pearl of great price. Psychologist Viktor Frankl reminds us that man is a striving animal and that taking responsibility *for his life* is the very essence of existence. What is this "self" for which we are responsible and to which we must relate in Jesus' way? Actually, it is our body, memory, imagination, reasoning, ability, and so on; in short, it is all of those things which are blended together to make up what is meant when one says, "I."

A Christian must learn *how* to relate creatively to all the different facets of selfhood in terms of what he believes; or he will, insofar as he fails, be less than the person he could be. To take one facet of selfhood as an example, consider the challenge that faces so many Christians in relating in Jesus' way to the physical side of being.[6] Those who live in white skins do not understand the adjustment that must be made by those who live in black ones. Healthy people are little aware of the problems that confront the sick, crippled, and deformed folk. The attractive know little of the adjustment problems that confront the unattractive. This is the way physician Paul Tournier sees it: "Many people will not accept their own bodies. No one knows the secret torment, often childish, but capable of turning into a regular obsession, that can be caused by a nose that is too long, legs that are too thick, by being too tall or too short, by a tendency to plumpness or an unharmonious voice. In short, by revolt against not being as handsome or as beautiful as one would like." (10)

Did you ever ask yourself what kind of person you would be if you had inherited a different kind of body? It is a sobering question. I always want to salute an individual who lives healthfully in a sick body—who has soul freedom in a physical prison. Or, consider the animal drives and instincts that environ our spirit. To these, also, we must relate in Jesus' way. Here we may live a little lower than either the angels or the animals.

Memory, reason, and imagination will be examined later, but suffice it to say here that a Christian *must* be constantly on guard lest he become a victim of inferior relatedness in dealing with any or all facets of selfhood.[7] He will not forget that Jesus is THE WAY.

Relating to Others

A Christian must relate to others in Jesus' way. People are important in the creating of persons. "If one cannot function in a significant way within his community," says Dr. Robert Leslie, "if he is driven to feel alienated and isolated from his community, then he will find status in ways that stand over against the community that first rejected him. . . . So, Zacchaeus, trying to protect a tottering self-esteem, departed his own people and threw in his lot with the hated conquerors." (11)

Harold Strong, as director of Children's Village at Dobbs Ferry, New York, held the opinion that the child's desire to belong is the central factor in juvenile delinquency. He finds that children go from group to group until they find one that will accept them. If they feel rejected by the "good" group and accepted by the "bad" group, then they will conform to the behavior of the latter group.[8]

According to Jesus, in our relationship to people, we are in danger of failing on two counts: with those who *mistreat us,* and with those who *need us.*

Those who mistreat us. We must take care lest those who "step" on us do not also debase us. So great is this danger that "If you are offering your gift at the altar," said Jesus, "and there remember that your brother has something against you, leave your gift there before the altar and go; first be reconciled to your brother, and then come and offer your gift." (Matt. 5:23-24 R.S.V.)

There will also be those who will use you, revile you, and push you around. For these people, pray and go out of your way to help them. Indeed, if they compel you to go one mile, then go a second on your own. (Matt. 5:38-48) No matter what they do, do not stop forgiving them. (Matt. 18:21) Never fail to let them start over again in your feelings. Think of yourself as being blessed by their villainy. "Be ye therefore perfect, even as your

Father which is in heaven is perfect," (Matt. 5:48 K.J.) . . . even with those who mistreat you.[9]

Those who need us. There is no greater violation of the human fabric than that of failing those who need us. It is so easy to pass them by on the other side (Luke 10:29-37), veiling our actions with flimsy excuses.

If people need us, they come first. The laws of Sabbath observance are secondary to the healing of a withered hand. (Matt. 12:12) For Christians, the concern for persons who need them is not unlike that of the saint who could not get warm until the dying beggar outside his door was covered. Christians feel a closeness to all human needs. No matter what prison other persons are in, be it the prison of race, ignorance, or prejudice, Christians will come unto them. (Matt. 25:31-46)

The mature person knows that he must think about others as he would have them think about him. Indeed, the person who relates to others in Jesus' way will seek for the socially, psychologically, economically, and spiritually lost. Jesus represented God as seeking man, even as a good shepherd seeks for a lost sheep or a poor woman seeks for a lost coin. The true follower of Jesus is, of necessity, a fisher of men.[10]

Relating to Conditions   (Situations and Things)

A Christian must not only relate to God, self, and others, but he must also relate to conditions about him in Jesus' way. Paul said he had learned that whatever condition he was in, therein to be content. (Phil. 4:11) He had learned that even though he could not handle everything, there was no situation where he could not handle himself.

A young mother tells of how she had, through childhood and youth, come to think that life was a matter of doing good, placing it before God, and in return receiving God's blessing. Then her husband informed her that a business venture had failed and that they were greatly in debt. He went on to say that his moral principles would not let him take bankruptcy, but rather he would have to pay off dollar for dollar, no matter how long it took. She recalled seeing a small fish torn to shreds when dropped into a turtle tank, and she felt that their creditors were doing the same to her life and their future.

"Finally the day came when I felt I simply could not hold on one more day," she said. "I was changing a bunk bed, and I threw myself on it and cried as if my world had come to an end. Suddenly I found myself praying once again, but with a new and different faith.

" 'Please, God,' I begged, 'help me to accept this burden and to make the best of it.' I knew that I was ready to hand my problem over with no demands or pleases or complaints . . . it was not the end but a new beginning. We were entirely in God's keeping at last." (12)

She was now ready, working with God, to meet life as she found it, not just as she wanted it to be. A Christian has to learn how to do this in Jesus' way.[11]

Mrs. Plumb and I went on a European guided tour some years past. Finding money for it was no small achievement, but we felt (at least, we had so rationalized it) that it was worth the sacrifice. With eagerness we came to the ship for our first ocean voyage, only to find that, because of a strike, the ships had been "switched," and we were to go on an "old tub." We had to live in separate dormitories for the nine-day ocean trip! And that was not all. When we reached Europe, we were confronted with inadequate bus space for our large group and traveled with much discomfort.

I found myself deeply disturbed, saying to my wife, to myself, and to those about me, "This isn't fair." The thing that bothered me most was that this first and what we thought our last and sacrificial trip was being ruined. Then I remembered Paul's achievement, "For I have learned in whatever state I am, to be content." (Phil. 4:11) I have learned that when I cannot change the situation, I must handle myself. And I did.

Herbert Gray, an English preacher, once asked an old man if he would like to live life over if it would turn out exactly the same again. Gray did not expect the answer he was given.

"Yes," said the old man, "and especially would I like to live again through my times of trouble . . . because it was in these times that I learned most about God."[12] (13)

It can be that way, if we relate in Jesus' way to conditions about us.

Somewhere I read of a perfume factory messenger who took fragrance wherever he went. He was saturated with the odor of the place where he worked. Most of us give evidence of where we live, and this evidence is not always fragrant. Viktor Frankl, during his concentration camp experience, learned that "freedom is freedom to take a stand toward conditions, but it is not a freedom from conditions." (14)

As a young man Bishop Werner served a church in Saskatchewan, Canada. He made his home with a widow and her sixteen-year-old son, who lived in a 12-by-20 tar paper shack. The woman, he said, became his prairie mother. "I've never known anybody more queenly. By the miracle of her presence, a bare, rude shack was transformed into a lovely, happy home. . . . Where someone else would have rebelled or become bitter, she accepted life. She took life with all its disappointments and its impasses and made it beautiful." (15)

I think we would say that this dear lady was not mastered by her conditions but master of them. She was a living example of one who was not anxious about life, centering her concern on what she would eat or what she would put on, but was able to seek first things first.

To relate to conditions in Jesus' way is to cultivate the best in even the worst situations. It is to overcome the evil with the good.[13]

The Need for Balanced Relatedness

Concerning our definition of a Christian, it should be further pointed out that a well-balanced relatedness is the very essence of spiritual maturity. Someone asked Gene Tunney how he accounted for his success as a boxer. His answer was most revealing. He enumerated ten abilities needed by a good fighter—such as to be able to give abuse, to take abuse, and so forth.

"Now," he said, "I have never fought with a man that could not excel me in some of these areas, but I think my success was due to the better balance in which I used these abilities as compared to my opponent's." Some people are tempted to go all out for one area and pay little attention to the others. The only spiritual concern for some Christians is being saved—that is, relating to God. The "peace of mind" movement has drawn some sharp criticism, not because we do not all need "peace of mind," but because of the devotees' all-but-exclusive emphasis on relating to self. The "social gospel" belongs to Christianity as love to marriage, but to bring no more than love to marriage is to destroy it. Jesus had a dynamic relationship to others, *but* He had more. Living with conditions from poverty to affluence often separates the men from the boys. In relating to things, we may become an ascetic, a cynic, or a saint.

A Christian Relates in Jesus' Way in All Four Areas of Life

To relate to any one area at the exclusion of the others warps a Christian's effectiveness, just as the judgment of the blind men when they touched the elephant. Each area, in turn, must be kept in balance with the other three facets of Christian relatedness.[14]

We turn now to the foremost of all Christian questions. What is the spiritual dynamic of the Christian way of life? What makes our pursuit of spiritual truth and our efforts to relate in Jesus' way come alive? We are assuming that if we are going to relate in Jesus' way, we must have what Jesus had. What was it?

NOTES

1. On first reading, does this seem to leave anything out?
2. Do you agree with this? If not, what is greater than being a person at his best?
3. Make an acceptable restatement of the author's position on the significance of "relating."
4. What does the statement "Jesus is the way" mean to you— would you add anything to this?

5. See if you can agree on a restatement of the author's belief in the importance of relating in Jesus' way to God.

6. See if you can agree on a restatement of what the author means by "self." How many of you can agree with him?

7. How much of life's sorrows come from our failure to adjust to what we have or do not have—such as ability, appearance, personality, and the like?

8. How much does this account for the "hippy" group following? Does this not apply, in a large measure, to all of us?

9. This is a searching principle. How important do you think it is in our relating to others in Jesus' way? Can you give any examples?

10. Can one be a Christian and leave the social gospel out?

11. Give a personal illustration of this.

12. Are most people made less or more Christian in their relating to conditions?

13. What positive or adverse conditions would be most apt to throw you? How much would more or less money affect your spiritual quality?

14. What emphasis do you think needs the most attention in our time? Which of the four is getting the most emphasis now in your church? In the general church? Where does the racial issue come in this relatedness?

Part II

POWER TO BECOME

John 1:12

To be as Jesus is the first business of a Christian; but it must be obvious to all that no one can do this unless he has what Jesus had.

If I may be a bit facetious, it is related that in the days of mules and horses, a certain driver could not get his mule, which was all saddled for a trip, to budge. A veterinarian came by, noted the problem, and volunteered his assistance. It was readily accepted, and the doctor forthwith gave the mule a hypo. The mule stood still for a few seconds, wiggled a bit, and then took off like a jet. The owner stood there, both grateful and confused, then pleadingly asked the doctor, "Will you give me one of those shots? I have to catch that mule."

Jesus had the power "to become." That same power is not only available to us but it is also of first importance that we have it if we will "come after" him.

What is the nature of this empowering experience that enables a person to relate in Jesus' way to God, self, others, and conditions about him? And from where and why does the power come? Or, to say it another way, in the next two chapters we are taking a hard look at the so-called "warm heart" or religious experience. To do this, we are going to have to submit religion (yours and mine) to some careful analysis. We must passionately pursue truth and never try to defend some concept that has become sacred to us. We will have the confidence of any good artist that the more we understand the parts, the better we will be able to put them together into a creative and meaningful arrangement.

CHAPTER III

The Empowering Experience

OUR QUEST: *What is it, if present, that makes any Christian religion a vital force to its possessor but, if absent, leaves whatever is thought of as Christianity sterile and lifeless?*

Some years ago, I conducted a class concerned with understanding other religions, using speakers from various bodies of the Christian religion and a few non-Christians, such as a Jewish rabbi, a Zoroastrian, and a Mohammedan, added for seasoning. Their assignment was to acquaint the class with the good life as they saw it and to show them how they could get it. As much as possible, I interviewed them both before and after their presentations. I had, during my college and seminary days, courses in comparative religions, but this was deeper and different. These people impressed me by their sincerity, spiritual well-being, and ability. It was quite evident that their religions were effective in their lives.[1] It became clear then, and it has become increasingly clear through the years, that Christian religions have much that is superficial about them, and it is this which tends to hide from our view a common and dynamic force present in them all with varying degrees of effectiveness. This common force is the wheat,[2] and all else is chaff and straw. The latter serves its purpose in obtaining the wheat, but of itself it has no ultimate importance.

George Bernard Shaw was getting close to the facts when he said, "There is only one religion, though there are a hundred versions of it." After more than twelve years reporting the affairs of the churches for the Associated Press, covering national and international meetings and describing trends, positions, and the leadership of Protestant, Roman Catholic, and Orthodox groups, George W. Cornell wrote: "The point has been continually and inescapably driven home to me . . . they're cut from the same cloth. There is a common ground of faith, compatible and essentially undeviating, that runs through them all." (1)

By way of illustration, if all the different types of internal combustion engines were placed in a long row, starting with the smallest hobby airplane motor and proceeding to the largest gasoline engine made, they would differ radically in appearance and in power production. But the basic principle of *creating and harnessing an explosion* would be operative in and common to them all. The theories, theologies, and rituals of our various Christian religions can be compared to the machinery of our gasoline engines. They, too, are but the means by which a power is created and harnessed. Just as the creative mind of man has worked out many ingenious ways to create and harness an explosion, so has it discovered quite as many ways to create and harness the force which is common to all Christian approaches; and therewith he has given us our Christian denominationalism and, in a large measure, other religious groups.

A Quaker in the silence of his meetinghouse and a Roman Catholic with his dramatic processions and ritual are a long way apart in their practices, but they do not need to be far apart in their experiences. It is quite evident that their differences are as superficial as is the stove used in cooking a meal (gas, electric, coal, or wood) or the kind of dishes in which it is served; certainly it is the taste and quality of the food that counts.

One is reminded of Charles Lamb's story of the roast pig. A Chinese, rummaging through the ashes of a recently burned house, inadvertently pushed his finger into the well-roasted flesh of a pig. He quickly stuck his burning finger into his mouth to cool it and obtained such a delectable taste that he ate the whole pig. After this, whenever he craved another roast pig, he forthwith burned down another house.

Whether one roasts a pig in an electric oven or by burning down a house, he has what is of first importance—the roast pig. So we find some Christians creating this spiritual dynamic in one way and some obtaining it in another. Some methods may be compared to the burning down of a house and others to the electric oven. Every devotee will decide which is which for himself. The important thing for us to see is that all effective Christians experience and harness a common and dynamic force, and it is here that our spiritual blurs come into focus.[3]

Faith as the Religious Dynamic

This common spiritual experience has been thought of in many and differing ways, but the word that best describes it is *faith*. Furthermore, it seems clear that the life and teaching of Jesus boldly support this conclusion. I appreciate that this word has kept confusing, not to mention sometimes bad, company. Many will say, "This is my faith," when what they really mean is, "This is what I believe." On other occasions, faith is treated as a kind of magic. May I ask you to objectively reexamine this word faith and how it is related to the common, dynamic Christian experience. I ask you to do this because no matter how many times I have sought for another word, I have always been forced to come back to it.[4]

Adolph Von Harnack, German Biblical scholar of note, is reported to have said that Jesus' teachings about faith were so simple that they could be understood by a child, yet so complex that the ablest mind found them incomprehensible. I am inclined to think that Jesus did make faith simple, and it is his followers who have made it complex.

Faith Concept Reexamined

The concept of faith has been confused, in part, by the failure to distinguish between faith and belief. Bishop Watkins makes the distinction between "saving faith," which involves commitment, and "intellectual faith," which does not. He then says, "Unfortunately, the English language does not permit an exact translation of the word that Paul uses for this act of commitment because in English, the noun 'faith' does not have a corresponding verb. The Greek language did have a verb for faith so that Paul could speak of 'faithing' God. All we can do in English is to resort to another word and to speak of 'believing' in God."[5]

(2)

Dr. William Hordern notes that Paul in Romans 6 makes it clear that man is "saved by a faith-relationship with Christ." Hordern's observations would go beyond Bishop Watkins; for, says he, "We know that in the later writings of the New Testament, the concept of faith as belief was already beginning to form. In James, we find an attack upon such a concept." (3) As James saw it, to believe was not enough. "Thou believest there is one God; thou doest well; the devils also believe and tremble." (James 2:19 K.J.)

Faith Defined

This faith which is common to all religions is a verb—not a noun—and is in no way synonymous with belief or believing. When we are faithing we are doing something quite different than when we are believing.

Let us begin our definition by saying that faith is a feeling, the opposite of fear.[6] If we can get a clear, concise definition of fear, we will have no trouble finding an equally luminous definition of faith. I think we are justified in saying that Jesus recognized fear to be the opposite of faith. Take, for instance, the storm incident. "Save, Lord; we are perishing," they said. And Jesus asked, "Why are you afraid, O men of little faith?" (Matt. 8:25 R.S.V.)

Fear may express itself in a number of ways, such as dread, apprehension, hate, resentment, jealousy, and panic. Faith, on the other hand, may manifest itself in trust, confidence, surrender, love, generosity, and the religious experience. The most dynamic and life-changing expression of fear, of course, is panic. And the most vital and life-altering expression of faith is the religious experience, as we shall observe. *To miss the feeling (faithing) side of religion is, actually, to miss religion.*[7]

Feeling the Facts

Both faith and fear are what we know, or think we know, emotionalized. No concept comes alive until we feel it. When we emotionalize a negative conclusion, we have fear; when we feel a positive one, we have faith. Faith is the substance of a hope (positive judgment). Fear is the substance of hopelessness (negative judgment).[8]

Francis Bacon had this in mind when he said that it is not the food we eat but the food we digest that gives us strength. In this same vein Herbert Spencer a number of years ago, in his *Social Statistics,* wrote that education alone never makes a man better. "Creeds pasted upon the memory, good principles learnt by rote, lessons in right and wrong will not eradicate vicious propensities. . . . If, in place of making a child *understand* that this thing is right and the other wrong, you make it feel that they are so . . . if, in short, you produce a state of mind to which proper behavior is *natural, spontaneous, instinctive,* you do some good." (4)

Truth is never effective (digested and turned into energy) until one faiths it or fears it. Let me illustrate with a newspaper account of an ash collector who inherited some $1,500,000. After a few days the reporters, in search of a human-interest story, looked him up. When they found him, what do you think he was doing? Celebrating? Buying a car? Buying new clothes? No, he was still on the job carrying ashes from his customers' basements and dumping them into his truck. The reporters gathered about him, clicked their cameras, and asked questions, wanting to know if he really had inherited this fortune. "Yes, yes," he answered with visible irritation and, returning to his ash collecting, warned, "If you don't stop this publicity, I will lose my customers."

It is quite evident that, though this man knew intellectually he had inherited a million and a half dollars, he did not feel it in his heart. He felt like an ash collector. The facts never got to his feelings. From the above statement one may sense how easy it is, religiously speaking, to be an intellectual theist (believer in God) and, at the same time, be an emotional atheist (not feeling God in what we do). There is a striking difference between intellectual and emotional acceptance of spiritual truth.

Martin Luther told this story about himself. "When sorely bereft by the wickedness of the world and the dangers besetting the church, and seeing my wife dressed in mourning, I asked the reason. 'Do you not know,' she said, 'that God is dead?' I explained how God cannot be dead; that he is immortal and will live immortally. 'And yet,' she said sorrowfully, 'you are so hopeless and discouraged.' And I mastered my sadness."

This was, of course, Luther's wife's way of calling to His Venerable's attention that, though his reason was theistic, his emotions were atheistic. He believed in God, but he did not faith him. He intellectually accepted God, but he did not feel God in his everyday life. A further emphasis on the importance of faithing (feeling) what we believe is found in the life of Adoniram Judson, who gave his life as a Christian missionary in Burma. In his work as a missionary, he accepted and taught that man was immortal; but when his wife died, he gave up his work and spent most of his time lying on her grave, caught in the grips of deep mourning. This continued for so long a time that his friends became deeply concerned and, in desperation, one of them daringly told Judson that he was behaving like a pagan—meaning, of course, that though he accepted immortality intellectually, he had not done so emotionally. Though he believed like a Christian, he felt like a pagan. The shock treatment worked. Judson got back on the job. The great missionary must have immediately understood what had happened to him; for when he went out as a missionary, he asked the people at home to pray that "I not lose the *life* of religion in my soul."

"The problem with Protestants," says Dr. Harry Emerson Fosdick, "is not that they think of God as untrue, but rather as unreal. It is one thing to believe in God, and it is another thing to confront him." We will never confront God in what we think, but only in what we feel. It was out of experience that John Wesley called faith a "disposition of the heart." Before Aldersgate, he had truth known; after it, he had truth felt. William James observed this and remarked, "For some, religion is a dull habit while for others it is an acute fever." And so it is.[9]

Interpreting the Faithing (Religious) Experience

No small amount of our religious estrangement has grown out of the way we have interpreted the religious (faithing) experience. In reading William James' book, *Varieties of Religious Experience*, the "varieties" do not seem so much in the experiences but in the interpretation. "We must help men identify and authenticate their spiritual experience," says Bishop Gerald Ensley. "We shall not get far by attacking science or scientific method; we are too much its debtor for that. What we must insist on is that there is no one single, incontrovertible line of evidence for the nature of Reality, not even the scientific. The fact that I look out of my window and see the sun rise in its glory does not mean that my neighbor, in order to see it, must come into my chamber and look out my window." (5)

Not only may each of us have a true and bona fide religious experience in our own "religious chamber," but we are almost certain to interpret that experience according to our own theological bias. Let us take the case of Jeanne Chaix, as told by Dr. Harry Emerson Fosdick.

A century ago a French citizen left to the French Academy a fund which, increased by others, year after year furnishes prizes for conspicuous exhibitions of virtue discovered in the French population. Here is a typical case: Jeanne Chaix, the eldest of six children—mother insane; father chronically ill; she, with no more money than the wages she earns in the pasteboard factory where she works, brings up the family, maintains the entire household which, says the records, "subsists morally, as well as materially, by the sole force of her valiant will."

Doctor Fosdick goes on to say,

With these few facts, what do you know about Jeanne Chaix, standing there to receive her prize from the French Academy? You know this—she had not grown bitter; life had done hard things to her but she had not been embittered; she must have been sustained by an undiscourageable goodwill. She was a healthy-minded girl. Moreover, I suspect that, being French, she was a good Catholic too and that, more than once, when the burden did seem unjust and she was tempted to be bitter, she went up to the church and prayed to the Blessed Virgin and came down again sweetened and reinforced. (6)

One can certainly be justified in assuming that Jeanne Chaix had a religious experience of the highest order, and she inevitably interpreted it in terms of the Blessed Virgin. How difficult it would have been for her to have done otherwise. Peter was forced to interpret religious experience beyond his Jewish tradition, but not without shock. "Truly I perceive that God shows no partiality." (Acts 10:34 R.S.V.) And then he asks, "Can anyone forbid water for baptizing these people who have received the Holy Spirit just as we have?" (Acts 10:47 R.S.V.)

The objective interpretation of experience, religious or otherwise, never comes easily. Herbert Butterfield, in his introduction to Arthur Koestler's book, *The Sleepwalkers*, says ". . . all cosmological systems, from the Pythagoreans to Copernicus, Descartes and Eddington, reflect the unconscious prejudices, the philosophical or even political bias of their authors; and from physics to physiology, no branch of Science, ancient or modern, can boast freedom from metaphysical bias of one kind or another." (7) It is good to keep this well in mind while interpreting any experience, especially the religious experience.

There is an old Stoic axiom which asserts that men are torn by the opinions they have of things, rather than by the things themselves. How often people think they are divided from others by facts and experience, when really it is only the personally slanted interpretation of facts and experience that is pushing them apart and away from truth. Though much of religious experience is still warped by personally slanted interpretation, one needs to keep firmly in mind that such freedom as is enjoyed by the scientist of today, to pursue and interpret experience in terms of evidence rather than tradition, is a recent historical phenomenon. As evidence of this, consider Copernicus for a moment. This great man formulated what is virtually our present concept of a sun-centered cosmos. He set forth this revolutionary idea in less than twenty-five pages at the beginning of his book. (It represents about 5 per cent of his presentation.) The remaining portion of his book has to do with the application of this sun-and-star-centered theory, trying to show that this new idea fits into the "medieval framework based on Aristotelian physics and Ptolemaic wheels. It was like trying to fit a turbo-prop engine on a ramshackle old stage-coach." (8) But Copernicus spent the rest of his life, and the remainder of his book, tortuously trying to make a great insight fit into the concepts of the past—trying to put new wine into old bottles.

All too often, this is what is done with religious experience; and, not unlike Copernicus, it is done without any awareness of it. We force experience to identify with dogma.[10] (9) Dr. Wyatt Aikin Smart has facetiously pointed out that if we have red ink on our fingers when the religious experience comes to us, we are prone to think that no one can have a similar experience unless he, too, has red ink on his fingers.

Surely, the church must see that it is *the faith—the religious experience*—that is important and not the theological interpretation that the experiencer may give to it.[11]

SUMMARY

A Christian has been defined as one who relates to God, self, others, and conditions about him as he believes Jesus would relate if he were living in his time and place. We have seen that Christians (some would say, the followers of all religions) have a common and unifying force which, for lack of a better name, we have called "faith" (a state of feeling—the opposite of fear). We recognized the importance of beliefs, but noted that a belief that is not felt is as ineffective as a book not read. We also observed that fear, at its worst, is panic; faith, at its best, is the religious experience. Faith, like fear, may have many stimuli, but one tendency is evident: we are inclined to interpret our faithing experience in terms of the theology we hold, or heard at that time. Therefore, religious people do not so much present a "variety of religious experiences" as a variety of interpretations of religious experiences.

NOTES

1. Would it seem to you to be deprecating to the Christian religion if we were to find that all religions—Christian and non-Christian—use the same dynamic?

Without striving for a final answer, think on the question, What does a Christian have that a Jew does not? State your thinking in nontheological terms.

2. In a tentative way, spell out the chaff and the wheat of the Christian religion as you see it now.

3. Do all Christian approaches have the same dynamic? What is the author's view? What is your view?

4. Have you felt any confusion regarding the meaning of the word "faith"?

5. As you see it now, what is the relationship between "faithing" and "believing"?

6. If fear is not the opposite of faith, then what is?

7. Restate the author's view of faith and fear. What is the relationship of the religious experience to faith? To fear?

8. Can you agree on a restatement of the author's position on the relationship of faith and fear to reason?

9. Restate the author's distinction between truth known and truth felt. How would you state this observation?

10. In what way does a person's theology affect his religious experience?

11. What do we mean by "varieties of interpretation of religious experience"?

CHAPTER IV

What Does Faith Do?

OUR QUEST: *What part does faith, the Christian dynamic, play in man's effort to live in Jesus' way? What is its cosmic significance? In short, what makes faith so important?*

A review of the Gospels will make it evident to anyone that faith was a vital part of Jesus' ministry. When a certain woman touched the hem of Jesus' garment and became well, Jesus did not say to her, "I did it," or "God did it," but rather he said, "Daughter, *thy faith* hath made thee whole." (Mark 5:34 K.J.) On another occasion, Jesus was sought out by two blind men. He touched their eyes, saying, "According to *your faith* be it unto you." (Matt. 9:29 K.J.) We might extend this list of references for many pages, but the question is this: What did faith do that made the difference between sickness and health?[1]

The Physiologist's Answer

The physiologist thinks of faith as an important force in every man's search for health. I recall someone's relating the following experience. It seems that a man was in a hurry and, at the same time, caught in a slow-moving, long line of traffic. No risk seemed too great for him to take as he passed one car after another, forcing other drivers to make room for him so that he would not collide with them or the oncoming traffic. His nerves were taut, and his disposition was rapidly deteriorating into panic. Then he read this scrawled on the back of an old jalopy: "Go ahead and push. It's your ulcer!"

We all know of those who have developed ulcers, or worse, because they did not know how to be at their best when under pressure. Whether or not we have read W. B. Cannon's book entitled *Bodily Changes in Fear and Rage*, there are few among us who have not experienced such changes. We have seen our bodies become both victim and beneficiary of our emotional states.

As an illustration: Suppose you and several of your friends are having a picnic on the edge of an Alaskan woods. You are frying and eating bacon sandwiches. By now you have all eaten so much that courtesy runs high as you urge each other to take the last piece now frying in the pan. At this point a bear, who has been following the scent of the frying bacon, breaks into view. Each of your party makes a dash for safety. When you assay the situation three minutes later, two of you are up a tree and the other two are a block away. Just imagine running at top speed or climbing a tree on a full stomach! From where did this new strength for running and climbing come?

We need no help to see that it came from a change in emotions. When the bear appeared, fear took over, and the glandular secretions of your bodies were shifted from digesting food to creating super-strength to keep you from being the bear's food. It was all a matter of glandular secretion stimulated by fear. After the bear left, the glands came under the command of faith again. If, on the other hand, your fears had "kept you up the tree," as it were, your glands might well have poisoned your bodies to the point of making you sick.

From a strictly physiological standpoint, faith or fear is the main prescription-writing influence behind the glands. Whether one believes in God or not, he still has to have faith just to get along in his body. His health depends on it. He may not be a religious person, but if his stomach, his heart, and his blood vessels are to function normally, he must have faith. We have come to see that faith is all but as important as fresh air and good food. Our vitamin-fed bodies become easy prey to disease when the vital control which faith alone can supply has surrendered to fear.[2]

The Psychologist's Answer

For those interested in mental health, faith (as the opposite of fear) is a state of mind that enables us to be ourselves. Surely there is no man so free as the man who is free to be himself. Faith, and faith alone, gives him that freedom. The evils of fear can be mastered only by the blessings of faith. How many times have you said within yourself, "I could do better than he (or she) if only I were not afraid"? Maybe this person you were watching was acting as toastmaster, singing a solo, making a speech, telling a story, or leading a game. Jesus spoke of many when he told the parable of the man who hid his talents because he was afraid. (Matt. 25)[3]

Yes, if faith were no more than "positive thinking," it would still be, physiologically and psychologically speaking, indispensable in our search for health.

Some Religious Answers

The religious answer to our question, What does faith do? is our chief concern.

Let us begin with Tolstoy's observations, "Faith is the force of life." Mark records Jesus as using faithing both to curse and to destroy. (Mark 11:12-14) At other times he quotes him as accrediting to faith the power to remove mountains, saying in effect that where there is faith, there is power. (Mark 11:23) The question confronting us is, How is faithing related to this power? Does faith create, channel, or ground this power in life? What does faith do?[4]

As we turn to consider a number of different answers to our question, let us keep in mind that each of them is *the* answer for someone. May this presentation help you to find the answer *for you.* With whom you agree, or disagree, is not important.[5]

Faith as Qualifying Us for God's Favor

Some religious people look upon faith as a means by which they qualify themselves for God's power and favor. Faith, to them, is a kind of currency. They think of the shelves of God's heaven as bulging with the many good things they need in order to have a paradise on earth. God has set a price on each of these items, such as moral quality, trust, or faith. When they meet God's price, he lets them have it, and not until then. Meeting

God's condition is man's only responsibility. As Theodore Cuyler put it: "God does not give us ready money; he issues promissory notes, and then pays them when faith presents them at the throne. Each of us is given a check-book." Sometimes faith presents the promissory note through an act of obedience, as did the father whose daughter was given but a few hours to live. In spite of what the physician said, he knew that his daughter could live if he, the father, would give up the manufacturing business and enter the Christian ministry. According to his testimony, from the time he told God that he would do His will, the daughter began to get well, and in a short time she had completely regained her health. This man was convinced that had he not surrendered to God's will, his daughter would have died. We might, in this case, be led to think of God as having omnipotent power to draw on but refusing to enter healingly into the girl's body until he could have his way with her father—unless the father would meet certain conditions.

For many, this view does not seem to be worthy of a Father God. They would not question but that the girl would have died if the father had not prayerfully surrendered. What they do question is the interpretation of *why*.

Dr. William Stidger, while pastor at Morgan Memorial in Boston (the original of the Goodwill Industries), came to his office after being at the hospital where his daughter, Betty, was still under anesthesia following an operation. Brother Benbury, a fellow minister, came quietly into the office, making sympathetic inquiry about Betty, and Stidger cried and choked a bit in response to his sincerity. Seeing this, Benbury got down on his knees and, after his formal introduction, prayed "straight from the shoulder" something like this: "Now, Lord God Almighty, see here now. Betty is up there in the hospital still under ether, and Brother Stidger is worried. Brother Stidger is your preacher and has been sticking by you for a long time (Benbury banged his hand on the table at this point); now you have got to stick by him, and no monkey business, Lord. Amen. Amen."

This may seem a bit unorthodox, but if we will be honest, Brother Benbury was expressing, in an unvarnished way, the real attitude of a lot of people when they are praying. "I have, by faithful obedience, created a balance in God's bank and He will not let my checks (prayers) bounce."

In the October, 1961, issue of *Together* magazine there is an article on Billy Sunday. It seems that he was holding revival meetings at Galesburg, Illinois. The meetings were so successful that the football games at nearby Knox College were getting very little patronage. When he gave a chapel talk at Knox College, the author of the article, T. H. McClure, said that he managed to explain the predicament to the great evangelist. Billy responded, "You keep on with your games, Mac, we'll figure something out. Tell your team to come down to the tabernacle Friday night."

They did. The tabernacle was jammed. Billy rose for his final prayer, and this is how he prayed: "Now, God," he said, respectfully but confidently, "I want you to do a favor for some young friends of mine. Tomorrow we are going to have a football game here between Knox and Monmouth. The Knox boys say they need a full house to pay expenses and to put a little extra cash in the treasury. Please, God, give them a good crowd and make sure they have good weather and put on a good show for everybody. And God, I'm going to kick off. Please don't let me stumble. Thank you."

It is quite evident that Billy Sunday, as an evangelist, felt that he had met some conditions which gave him a right to expect some special favors from God.

For those who think of faith as qualifying for favor—to go to God without faith, whether with words or acts, would be like going shopping without money, but if we have money (enough faith), we can have as our very own anything that God has, from health to fortune. As money is negotiable personality in the affairs of men, so faith, according to this view, is negotiable personality in dealing with God. Faith "talks" with God. A person without faith is a pauper.

There is one point of difference, according to this view. The merchant needs our money in order to replenish his stock, but God does not need our faith. It does nothing for Him whatsoever and has no relationship to the things for which we seek. God simply requires it for our good or *by his nature.*[6]

Faith as Personalizing God's Power

Frank Laubach, the world's greatest missionary to the illiterate, thinks of the Holy Spirit as the love of Christ everywhere at once. Others would say that it is God's love, as demonstrated in the life of Jesus, available to all men. Whatever this God-given power is called (Grace, Holy Spirit, Presence), it is there for us, and the only way we get it is through faith. The question is, How does faith make God's power, or Holy Spirit, present in our lives?[7] There are many different answers.

The channel view of faith. Here is an air-tight box sitting in the sun. Inside, it is pitch dark. I drill a hole through its thick walls and the light rushes in and dissipates the darkness. What that hole is to the light of the sun, so is faith to the power of God; it is the channel by which God gets into our lives; only the size of the channel will limit the amount of God we receive.

The vessel view of faith. The size of the vessel will fix the amount of rain-water we capture; so the larger our faith vessel, the more we receive of God's "showers of blessings." One may be confronted by all the waters of the thundering Niagara, but the water he takes away will not exceed the size of his vessel.

The radio view of faith. In this view, God is to be compared to a powerful broadcasting station sending forth his spirit-radiance everywhere at all times. By faith the mind of man tunes in to God's wave length. God, the source of all power, does not arbitrarily say "yes" to one person and "no" to another, but each man gets according to his attunement. God's wave length is the same in all parts of the world for everybody. Those who tune in by faith will receive, and they will receive for just as long as they remain tuned in.

Faith as the Cosmic Creative Instrument

A creator must have some means of creating—and *God uses faith.* It seems reasonable to think of God as using faith. As the author of Hebrews put it, "By faith we understand that the world was created by the word of God so that what is seen . . . was made out of things which do not appear." (Hebrews 11:3 R.S.V.) All that is began in the hope of God, and then came to pass through God's faithing. (Hebrews 11:1)

The universe is visible testimony of how the creative power of mind, through faith, can create substance out of spirit and atoms out of ideas. God is drawing all things to perfection by his faith. In evolution we see the response of the principle of life to God's faith. God holds all things in the all-embracing and timeless grasp of his faith. Faith is God's creative instrument.[8]

Man also uses faith as a creative instrument. By faith he uses these same basic creative laws of the universe that God used and is using. God uses them in a big way; man, in a very small way; but both use them. The law of gravity does not just apply to one mass and not to another. While the sun is drawing the earth, the earth is also drawing the sun. For that matter, while the earth is holding you to its bosom, you are holding the earth to yours by this same law of gravity. The law of magnetism operates in ratio to the size and density of the mass, no matter what the mass is. In like manner, the creative principle of the universe could not be—and is not—limited to God's mind, but is used by all minds in ratio to their depth and quality (or however we may describe the "size" of a spiritual being).[9]

By faith man not only brings his own creativity to bear at the point of his prayerful concern, but he also focuses the creativity of God at this point. C. H. Dodd, in his book *The Bible Today*, says, ". . . whatever we may make of particular 'miracles,' the miracle-stories as a whole are saying precisely this—that where Jesus was, there was some incalculable and unaccountable energy at work for the dispersal of evil forces and the total renewal of human life; and this was nothing less than the creative energy of the living God." (1)

"The gospels certainly are not responsible," writes Paul Tillich in his book *The New Being*, "for this disappearance of power in the picture of Jesus. They abound in stories of healing; but we are responsible, ministers, laymen, theologians, who forgot that 'Savior' means 'healer'—he who makes whole and sane what is broken and insane, in body and mind." (2)

This creative power of God, used so effectively by Jesus, embraces all things. The dog, the flea, the bug, and the ant, quite as much as men, were and are created by him. Among men this creative power of God equally embraces the good and the evil, the just and the unjust. Man, like Jesus, can have more of this creative power in his life because, unlike the dog or ant, he can faith. Man may live like an ant or like Christ. It is all a matter of faithing.

Man's faith personalizes the power of God in human experience. God is always doing as much as love can do; he needs our prayer (a prayer is faithing with God) that more may be done.[10] In a true sense God can only help those who help themselves and as much as they help themselves. Jesus said, "Give, and it will be given to you; good measure, pressed down, shaken together, running over. . . ." (Luke 6:38 R.S.V.)

When we faith, we are focusing the creative energy of God at the point of our concern and thereby extending God's means of helpfulness We have no adequate illustration of this, but the relationship of a magnifying glass to the sun may be suggestive. The sun is shining with equal warmth on each of three piles of leaves. We move a magnifying glass over the second pile, and soon it is aflame. The same sun, but focused, made more personal, creates a fire. If the magnifying glass had been not just a passive glass but a unit of creative energy, we would be close to what faith does in man's relationship to God. *Man's faith gives forth power and is, at the same time, a catalyst for the power of God.*[11]

Why Faith Fails or Succeeds

We can see by this that failure and success in our faithing are basically power problems. We can hardly expect fifty units of faith power to succeed over one hundred units of resistance. Part of this power comes from our faith and part (the much greater part) from the focusing of God's creativity, but the amount of creative power that will be at any one place is dependent upon the depth, length, and breadth of *our* faith. *God is always doing all he can.*[12]

"O Lord God, when thou givest to thy servant to endeavor any great matter," said Sir Francis Drake in the sixteenth century, "grant us to know that it is not the beginning but the continuing of the same until it is thoroughly finished which yieldeth the true glory." True prayer is not just being there but being there *in* faith until it is finished. It is being there *with enough* and *on time.*

Jesus put it this way: "For which of you, desiring to build a tower, does not first sit down and count the cost, whether he has enough to complete it? Or what king going to encounter another king in war, will not sit down first and take counsel whether he is able with ten thousand to meet him who comes against him with twenty thousand." (Luke 14:28-31 R.S.V.)

We must exercise no less wisdom in prayer—our faithing with God. Indeed, with faith, as in few other areas, we need to cover our investments with greater investments if we will avoid failure. James is right when he says that the prayer of faith will save the sick (James 5:15), but we must not think of prayer as a magic wand of some kind. The prayer of faith saves the sick by reason of creative strength. Any little passing creative prayer (faithing) will not save a person with a well-established chronic trouble.

Jesus, Peter, James, and John had just returned from the mountaintop experience, and there came a man who fell on his knees before Jesus and besought him.

Lord, he said, have mercy on my son for he is an epileptic and he suffers terribly; for often he falls into the fire, and often into the water. And I brought him to your disciples, and they could not heal him.

And Jesus answered, O faithless and perverse generation, how long am I to be with you? How long am I to bear with you? Bring him here to me. Then Jesus rebuked him, and the demon came out of him, and the boy was cured instantly.

Then the disciples came to Jesus privately and said, Why could we not cast it out?

He said to them, Because of your little faith. For truly, I say to you, if you have faith as a grain of mustard seed, you will say to this mountain, Move hence to yonder place, and it will move; and nothing will be impossible to you. (Matt. 17:14-20 R.S.V.)

If we have enough faith, nothing is impossible to us, but if we have little faith, only the little is possible for us. If this man's son had had just a slight trouble, the disciples may well have healed him with great ease.

We "pray and not faint" because we know our success will always be equal to our strength, not because our prayers are 100 percent successful. Jesus prayed for Judas, and yet Judas betrayed him. But this would no more have caused Jesus to stop praying (faithing with God) than you would consider giving up electric power just because a one-fourth-horsepower electric motor that you had on hand would not do a two-horsepower job. You would know that it was not the electricity that was at fault, but that you did not have the ability to harness the electricity in sufficient quantity to do the task at hand.[13]

Faith and Moral Evil

If we accept the creative concept of faith, we see clearly that a large portion of the moral evil of the world may well be the product of man's negative use of his creative power (faithing or fearing against God).

A vessel of water, as seen from above, may serve to illustrate our point (compare next page.)

We have here a piece of steel held up by cork and floating on the water at point *B*, a large magnet at point *C*, and a small magnet at point *A*. The large magnet at point *C* is fixed as to both location and drawing power. The magnet at point *A* may operate anywhere from A to C. It may operate anywhere from complete opposition to complete cooperation with the large magnet C.

Let us call the central piece of steel B the point of prayer

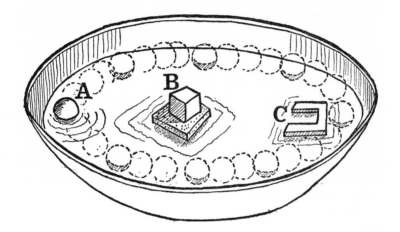

concern. The large magnet at point C symbolizes God, and the roving magnet at point A represents man. God is, at all times, drawing all things unto himself as much as he possibly can. Man, too, has magnetic creative powers even as God, only much, much, much less. With his faith-creating magnetism man can move anywhere from A to C—from being completely against God (devil man) to completely with God (Christ man). Prayer is faithing with God. When A becomes one with C, that is prayer. Prayer is the highest and noblest form of faithing.

Much of God's creative good will is used to neutralize the evil creativity of man. We live in a democratic universe. We shall always have what the majority, in the use of their creative strength, produce. To those who believe that God gives us power only to do what we ought to do and not what we want to do, we would say, rather, that this divinity of ours can be used to do evil or do good. *The devil has been well spoken of as a fallen angel.* (Isaiah 14:12; 2 Peter 2:4; Jude 6) He always is![14]

When I was a boy, a man in a neighboring vicinity took an axe and murdered his entire family one night. It was a shocking tragedy. The same axe might well have been used by this man, on other occasions, to chop wood for cooking meals or to keep his family warm at their summer camp. But he used it to kill. So may we use our divinity, our creative power, to build up or to destroy—like a gód or like a demon.

Paul was portrayed as using faith-power negatively at Paphos of Cyprus on a certain sorcerer by the name of Bar-Jesus who withstood them. "But Saul, who is also called Paul, filled with the Holy Spirit, looked intently at him and said, You son of the devil, you enemy of all righteousness, full of all deceit and villainy, will you not stop making crooked the straight paths of the Lord? And now, behold, the hand of the Lord is upon you, and you shall be blind and unable to see the sun for a time. Immediately mist and darkness fell upon him and he went about seeking people to lead him by the hand." (Acts 13:9-11, R.S.V.)[15]

I heard a teacher dismiss this account as fictitious because he did not believe that God would give anyone such powers. This hardly faces the facts. Look out upon the world, and you will see physical and mental strength used for the most destructive purposes. Certainly, I repeat, if man can use his imagination to work out diabolical killing gadgets, there is no reason to assume he cannot use his spiritual creativity for destructive ends also. To think otherwise is like talking about the law of gravity working when a friendly airplane drops bags of sugar for the starving, but ceasing to take effect when an enemy plane disgorges bombs on a hospital. It will be a rich day for humanity when man accepts his creative responsibility for a moral order—when he comes to see that man's creativity carries with it responsibility.

> Truly, I say to you, whatever you bind on earth shall be bound in heaven, and whatever you loose on earth shall be loosed in heaven. *(Matt. 18:18 R.S.V.)*

Jesus was speaking to all men, not just to Peter, in this case. This is a hard observation but must be frankly faced. We must see that the end of life is not just to have faith but, like Jesus, to use it in a constructive way.

No one has ever found a completely satisfactory answer to the problem of evil, but this is consistent with the creative view of faith.

We Need Not Agree

You may, or may not, find any of the above answers to the question, What does faith do? acceptable to you. This is not necessary. I do pray, however, that you will find one satisfactory to you. For again, no matter how much we differ with others as to *what faith does*, we are in agreement, I am sure, that we *must have faith* if we are to relate in Jesus' way to God, self, others, and conditions about us.

NOTES

1. Restate the question that confronts us.
2. Restate what faith does physiologically—as the author sees it; as you see it.
3. If a yardstick represented your abilities, how many inches are you free, through faith, to use—and how much is tied up with fear? How about the average person?
4. Our question is, What does the faithing experience in its varying expressions do? Does this seem important to you?
5. How important is it that we have the same answer to the question, What does faith do?
6. Restate this answer to our question, What does faith do? Do you know any who have this view? What are its good points—what are its weak ones?
7. Please see if you can restate the implication of this paragraph before you go farther.
8. Restate this view. What are your reactions to it? Where does this fit, or not fit, into the Genesis or evolution concept of creation?
9. Does this seem plausible to you? Why?
10. This seems a bit casual, but note carefully: "prayer is faithing with God."
11. Restate this concept of a personal God and compare it with some other views. Which view fits best with the cosmic scene as you see it?

12. Can you conceive of any reason why an earthly parent would withhold anything from his child that he needed for his health? Does not love have to do all it can, all the time, to be love? Think around this a bit.

13. In what way does this limit God and Jesus?

14. Restate this view of the creative concept of evil and prayer.

15. Where does this fit into the idea of cursing?

Part III

THE PATHS
THAT LEAD TO FAITH

We have defined a Christian as one who relates in Jesus' way to God, self, others, and conditions about him, and have agreed that, in order to do this, he must have the same faith-enabling power as had Jesus. We have surveyed the question of what faith does, and we trust that you have an answer that satisfies or is, at least, a working basis for you.

Our present concern is, from where and how do we get faith? Is it a gift or an achievement? It is our thesis that it is an achievement, and that there are two paths that lead to it—reason and experience. We shall explore both of them with great care.

CHAPTER V

Believing and Feeling

OUR QUEST: *We are concerned with the origin of our Christian beliefs and how our believing is related to the feeling side of our religion.*

The Source of Our Faith

Before we examine the relationship of belief to faith, it may be good for us to consider briefly the source of our faith—where do we get this spiritual dynamic? That is, does man receive faith (and also fear) as a gift from God, or is it an achievement?

> In Paul's First Letter to the Church at Corinth, he writes . . . there are varieties of gifts but the same spirit . . . and there are varieties of working . . . to each is given the manifestation of the Spirit for the common good. To one is given the utterance of wisdom; to another the utterance of knowledge . . . to another faith, by the same spirit; to another gifts of healing . . . all these are inspired by one and the same spirit who apportions to each one individually as *he* will. *(Cor. 12:4-11 R.S.V.)*

Some interpret Paul as saying that faith is one of God's many possible gifts to man, and he alone determines who is to be the recipient. This view is consistent with Paul's belief in election that some are predestined to be saved and others are predestined to be damned. Salvation is completely in God's hands.

The predestinarians tried to trap George Gordon, of the New South Congregational Church in Boston, on the night of his installation, by referring to the man whose withered hand was healed through the ministrations of Jesus, and asked, "Who healed this man's hand? Did this man do it or did God do it?"

Gordon answered, "Well, he had a hand in it."

To many of us, it would seem that if God gives faith, then, in a real sense, man does not have a hand in anything that is done. Is it not more consistent with experience to think of both fear and faith not as gifts but as achievements? We are endowed with the ability to think, and we are free to use it or misuse it. We have the capacity to remember, and we are free to cultivate it or neglect it. So do we have the capacity to fear or to faith.

As we probe to the greater depths of this spiritual dynamic that is common to all Christians, we proceed with the assumption that faith (and fear) is achieved; that faith is not like the pearl of great price that can be transferred from another to me for a price, as a commodity, but rather it is something that is accomplished through the use of a faculty—like a skill. Surely, if we do not have control at the point of faith, then the Gospel is a mockery. Indeed, we could not preach, Come, "whosoever will," but rather, Come, "whosoever can."[1] (1)

Let us now consider the relationship of "believing" to the faith experience.

Faith Is Rooted in Belief

Since both faith and fear are beliefs emotionalized, it follows, as the night the day, that believing comes before faithing.

Belief is to faith (and to fear, for that matter) what soil is to a plant. Remove the soil, or the quality of it, and the plant will wither. Remove the belief, or the quality of it, and faith will weaken or die. One cannot have faith in God or in himself unless he first believes in God or in himself. To destroy a person's belief in anything is to destroy his ability to have faith in it. The psalmist saw that if his beliefs were washed out, he would be "washed up." He testified that he would have fainted had he *not believed* to see "the goodness of the Lord in the land of the living." (Psalms 27:13 R.S.V.)

The account of Jesus walking on the water recorded by Mark and Matthew is not the occasion for many sermons in these days, yet there is something intensely interesting about it from the standpoint of the relationship of belief to faith. Jesus had left the disciples and had gone away for a season of prayer. In his absence the disciples took a boat and went out into the sea to do a little fishing, or maybe a little resting, all on their own. It is recorded that Jesus, returning from his prayer vigil and, seeing them some distance from the shore, walked to them on the water. (Most of us have not experienced a prayer session quite as vital as that.)

The disciples saw him and thought he was a ghost, but Jesus spoke to them and said, ". . . it is I; have no fear." And Peter answered him, "Lord, if it is you, bid me come to you on the water." He said, "Come."

"So Peter got out of the boat and walked on the water and came to Jesus; but when he saw the wind, he was afraid, and beginning to sink he cried out, Lord, save me. Jesus immediately reached out his hand and caught him, saying to him, O man of little faith, why did you doubt?" (Matt. 14:23-31 R.S.V.) A doubt (disbelief) leaves us with little faith— no matter where we walk.

Belief is basic. *One may have belief without faith, but he cannot have faith without belief.*

In John 1:12 we read, "But as many as received him, to them gave he power to become the sons of God." Bishop Hazen G. Werner says he prefers to translate it: "To as many as believed— to them gave he the power to become what they have dreamed of being." (2) Belief is the first step in receiving the power to become. James saw clearly that, before faith, there must be belief. No one can live a life of faith in God, Jesus, immortality, and so forth, unless he first believes in them. (James 2:14-26; James 5:15)[2]

Beliefs Are Reason-made

When we say that beliefs are reason-made, we are well aware that, for many people, reason is held suspect in the area of religion. Reason is to be trusted in the field of science but not in the area of religion, because religious truth comes through subjective insight, they say. The scientific method of objective research has no place in either the discerning or the evaluation of religious truths. Let me illustrate this fear of reason in religion by a personal reference.

While in high school, I felt that I should give my life to full-time Christian work. A district Interdenominational Sunday School promoter, passing through our town in the exercise of his duties, heard of my decision. Seeking me out, he said, "I hear you are going into the Christian ministry. What are you going to do when you finish high school?"

With a sense of pride, I daresay, I answered without hesitation, "I am going to go to college."

His immediate warning was, "Better not do that. You will lose your religion."

Well, I went to college, and near the time of my graduation I happened to be walking on the campus with a college official who was also a minister. In the course of our conversation he said, "I hear you have chosen the ministry."

"Yes," I replied.

"Where are you going to take your seminary work?" was the immediate and, I am sure, premeditated inquiry. I told him.

"Better not go there," he warned with visible feeling. "That is a very liberal school. If you go there, you will lose your religion."

It is very evident that both of these men were trying to tell me that my beliefs would not withstand the intellectual scrutiny of reasoning, and they also knew that if my beliefs crumbled, so would my faith.

I tell these experiences not because they are exceptional, but because they are all too common. The question that intrigued me then and has ever since, is this: Why should a prospective religious leader be so afraid of intellectual exposure? Is not such advice just as unworthy when given to a prospective clergyman as it would be to a prospective scientist?

Some years ago Sir Arthur Eddington, the British astronomer, said that there were those who were trying to prove, or disprove, that the wave length of light has no constant connection with the linear scale of its source. Now, if this were true, he said, it would involve a conception of atomic structure so far removed from that of the present-day quantum theory that scarcely anything of our present-day knowledge would survive. In laymen's language, he is saying that should anyone discover that light deteriorates by time and space, then most of our astronomical knowledge, so-called, would evaporate.

In the face of this, try to imagine some scientist saying to a student of science, "Don't listen to those men who are examining the relations of light and space to time, because if you do, you may come to some conclusions that will upset much of what we now hold as true. In fact, by listening to them you may even be led to give up scientific studies and turn to some other type of work."

A moment's reflection will lead anyone to see the absurdity of such advice when given to a prospective scientist. It would seem that this absurdity should be equally apparent when given to a student of religion. Surely true religion welcomes the full use of reason in the pursuit of truth. If reason cannot be trusted in the evaluation of all experience, then how can it be trusted with any experience? Simply to select the areas where reason is, or is not, to be trusted would presuppose the trustworthiness of reason itself.

It always seems a bit senseless to write long books and make long speeches trying to prove that something is right or wrong by the reasoning processes, and then to say in the next breath that you cannot trust reason. *The fact still remains that if reason had not established beliefs in the first place, then reason could not undermine and destroy them in the second place.* Paul admonishes Timothy, "Avoid such godless chatter for it will lead people into more and more ungodliness, and their talk will eat its way like gangrene. Among them are Hymenaeus and Philetus who have swerved from the truth by holding that the resurrection is past already. They are upsetting the faith of some." (2 Tim. 2:16-18 R.S.V.) What Paul called "godless chatter" was a form of reasoning that was undermining their beliefs and thus destroying the faith that rested upon them. Certainly if Paul had not, by reason, established their belief, then Hymenaeus and

Philetus could not have, by reason, swerved them from the "truth." To be sure, reason will be totally wrong some of the time and partially wrong most of the time, and yet we must turn to reason—and reason alone—for the evaluation of our experiences, be they experiences of God or of things.

Anyone whose beliefs are not sufficiently well grounded to stand intellectual scrutiny will do well to fear reason. It is this group that John Keats may well have had in mind when he said, in his "Ode to the Nightingale," "This world is a place where but to think is to be full of sorrow." It is reason that gives us our beliefs, and it is reason that will take them away unless they are undergirded by the most unimpeachable evidence available.

I conducted in my church a course called "Faith and Belief" each year for some twenty-five years. At the close of a recent session, a man in his mid-thirties said, "Thanks for the course; it has helped me no end. I am sure that I would be in the ministry today had I had this course in my early twenties. I was brought up in a religious home and the church, but what they taught me did not make sense over against what I was being taught at the university. I have remained in the church, saying and doing what I had been taught to say and do. What a relief to find that religion *is* reasonable; to see that whereas faith is the feeling side of religion, belief is—and must be—the intellectual side of it."

Indeed, "There is no honest retreat from rational thought into naïve belief" (3) in religion for those who dare to think honestly in all other aspects of life, for beliefs are reason-made.[3]

What Is a Belief?

By way of definition we might say that a belief is a conclusion to which the mind, because of various observations, has given the dignity of a fact. It is a conclusion which the reason has established as true, even though it does not have absolute, irrevocable evidence.

For instance, when I say I believe in God, I mean that I am intellectually satisfied that God exists. There is not enough evidence for me to call it a fact, but there is enough evidence for me to call it a belief. The importance of evidence in pursuing truth may be diagrammatically presented thus:

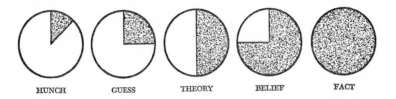

HUNCH GUESS THEORY BELIEF FACT

The shaded portions represent evidence. With little evidence, we have a hunch; by adding evidence, we have a guess; with still more evidence, we have a theory; with all but complete evidence, we have a belief; with final evidence, we get a fact. The adding and subtracting of evidence is always an intellectual process.

We Differ in Our Demand for Evidence

Was it not John Ruskin who said that some people catch opinions as others catch a cold? The difference between people in the area of their beliefs about any subject is not that one person has a belief with reason (examined belief) and another has a belief without reason (blind belief); it is rather that some demand more and others less evidence before they can accept anything as true, be it the virtues of a neighbor or the existence of God that is under consideration.

A layman in my church once said that he was not interested in theology. He did, in fact, seem to be a bit irritated when I brought it up, and he dismissed the whole matter by saying, "All the proof that I need I learned at my mother's knee." For him, as for many, the reason is satisfied if a priest, the church doctrine, a book, or early training and tradition says so, and he did not want to run the risk of more evidence.

Before Pope John, a Roman Catholic layman and friend put it this way: "I never argue about religion with my priest for the same reason that I never argue about medicine with my doctor. Doctors have studied medical science. I employ my physician to give me advice. If he is wrong and gives me the advice that leads to injury instead of health, then it is just too bad. So with the priest in our church. He has been educated in things religious. He says there is a God—a certain kind of a God, and if I do certain things I will be saved, and if I don't do them, I will be lost. I am taking his advice. Maybe he is wrong. If he is, it's just too bad."

My friend established his beliefs by reason, but used as the final evidence the word of the church passed on to him by the priest. J. Wesley Robb, author of *An Inquiry Into Faith,* says, "Faith becomes credulous when the presuppositions of any given religious approach to truth are accepted uncritically. This is equally true of dogmatic liberalism, dogmatic fundamentalism, dogmatic orthodoxy, dogmatic neo-orthodoxy or whatever." (4)

Some of us will want to go a step further and say that any faith that does not rest on carefully and critically examined presuppositions is apt to be more fancy than faith.

Those who must have much evidence before they can accept any proposition as true know that reason is not all there is to life, but they also know that it plays an important part in man's getting to the moon or to God. The warm heart must rest on intellectual integrity, and feelings must be clothed with knowledge; or, to quote Socrates, "We shall be better and braver and less helpless if we think we ought to inquire, than we should have been if we indulged in the idle fancy that there was no knowing and no use in seeking to know what we do not know." To insist that our beliefs be undergirded, with the best of evidence finds us, in the struggle between Abelard, the twelfth-century nonconformist theologian and penetrating thinker, and Bernard, Abbot of Clairvaux and political defender of tradition, on the side of Abelard, who pointed out that traditional authority was not enough to support faith, because authorities differ, but rather everyone must think it out for himself and thus depend on his own reason. (5)

In this connection, notice how Luther appealed to reason and evidence at his "trial." The prosecutor accused him formally of heresy and demanded a plain answer "without horns." Luther replied, "Unless I am shown by the testimony of Scripture and by *evident reasoning* . . . I am neither able nor willing to revoke anything, for to act against one's conscience is neither safe nor honest. God help me, amen!" (6)

When John Huss, the Bohemian reformer, was tried for his life, part of the evidence that was submitted against him was this passage taken from his writing: "The orders of popes, emperors, kings, princes and other superior personages are not to be obeyed unless they are founded on evidence and *reason*." It seems indisputable that belief-creating is the intellectual side of religion and that the amount and quality of the evidence we use in creating our religious beliefs are as important as they are in forming our scientific beliefs—just as subject to error and as replete with adventure.[4]

Vital Religion and Differing Beliefs

In his *Autobiographical Notes*, Einstein says, "Newton, forgive me, you found the only way which, in your age, was just about possible for a man of highest thought and creative power. The concepts which you created are even today still guiding our thinking in physics, although we know now they will have to be replaced by others farther removed from the sphere of immediate experience, if we aim at a profounder understanding of relationships." (7)

To follow Benjamin Franklin or Newton is not to do as they did, but to do in our time as they would do if they were living today. Certainly this is equally true of our efforts to follow Paul, Wesley, or Luther. We may well apply to religion the wisdom of Thomas Arnold, the English educator, who a century-plus ago said, "Two things we ought to learn from history; one that we are not in ourselves superior to our fathers; another that we are shameful and monstrously inferior to them if we do not advance beyond them."

We seem to be forced into one inescapable conclusion concerning beliefs; namely, that we do not have to have any particular interpretation of them to be a Christian. Paul's advice to

Timothy not to wrangle about words is as good today as when it was said. (2 Tim. 2:14) I do not have to have Paul's interpretation of Jesus in order to be a Christian, but I must have an interpretation that makes Jesus as real to me as he was to Paul, if I am going to be a Christian in my time. I do not have to have Augustine's concept of God, but I must have a concept that makes God as important to me as he was to Augustine. If I am going to follow Jesus, I do not have to accept the beliefs of St. Francis or of John Wesley, but I *must* have beliefs that are as intellectually acceptable to me as their beliefs were to them.[5]

Where Do We Get the Evidence?

The big question is yet to be considered. Where do we get the evidence, be it little or much, with which we establish religious truth? Does scientific evidence come in one way while religious evidence comes in quite another? I think not! In either case, we gather our evidence for establishing our beliefs through the critical examination of the data we get from our own and others' experiences. In science, one would be near the fact to say that the data come from the five senses (of self and others), whereas the data for establishing religious evidence come not only from the five senses but also from the sixth sense (intuitive awareness of self and others). *As matter is constantly acting upon our five senses, so is God ever acting upon our sixth sense, giving us data to interpret.*[6]

It is reported that when Phillips Brooks finally got the word "God" through to Helen Keller, she replied that she had always known about God but had not known his name. Calvin said, "We lay it down as a position not to be controverted that the human mind, even by natural instinct, possesses some sense of a Deity." (8) What we are saying is that this "sense of a Deity" constitutes a portion of the material used by reason to create religious beliefs.

It was Ghandi's firm belief that man is aware of God's direction in his life, but that this experience must come into the most careful scrutiny, for, said he, "If God has been in some of my decisions, he has made some dreadful mistakes!" (9) We must constantly test the spirit, lest we be misled by our interpretation of the evidence submitted by any and all of the "six" senses.

How differently we interpret the data that we get from our sixth sense (let alone the other five). Once Saul had some striking data presented to him on the Damascus road. It changed the course of his life. At the time of this experience, Saul was a Hebrew theologian trained under none other than Gamaliel. With this background, Paul (as God called "Saul") set forth to interpret both his sixth-sense experience and the life and death of Jesus. Let us suppose that, among the first theologically trained persons to interpret Jesus there had been an equally dramatically converted Zoroastrian or a Buddhist. Do we not have every reason to think that their interpretations of Jesus would have been much different from that of Paul, the Hebrew theologian? So do we have differing backgrounds as we come to the interpretation of the Christian beliefs, and, inevitably, come out with differing conclusions. This will become apparent if you are a part of a discussion group as you read Chapter VI on "Ways of Believing."

SUMMARY

Faith, we have seen, is achieved through the emotionalizing of beliefs. Belief is the soil for faith. Remove the soil and the plant will die. The belief soil is created by evidence through reason. Less than complete evidence is a belief; total evidence is a fact. A belief does not have to be true in order to support a rugged faith, but it must be true for the holder. Belief-creating is the intellectual side of religion and gathers its evidence not only from the five senses (as does science) but from the sixth sense as well.

NOTES

1. It would seem that either we are or we are not free beings. Restate these two views as clearly as possible.
2. Tie this statement and the emotionalizing of belief together.

3. Agree on a summary statement of this concept of the origin of beliefs.

a. What other view can one take?

b. Can you put the Pauline and this view together, or must we take one or the other?

c. What is your view?

4. What gives a belief quality?

How important is the quality of the belief to the quality of our faith?

Have you known anyone who lost their faith because their supporting beliefs collapsed?

5. In what sense must a belief be true before it can be the soil for faith: true for the person who has it—or scientifically true?

6. Restate the view here presented that spiritual truth comes from the interpretation of experience both intuitive and sensual.

Compare this with the platonistic view of revelation (we do not find truth—it is given to us). You may want to do a little extra reading here. Which view has been the historic view of the church?

Would not many scientists want to include the sixth-sense evidence along with that of the five?

CHAPTER VI

Ways of Believing

OUR QUEST: *To make an objective reexamination of the Christian beliefs.*

In this chapter we are listing the Christian beliefs in outline form without chronological importance, and under each of them are noted a number of the different concepts held by Christian people. Please check the concept under each belief which you most nearly accept, or write out another more suitable to you. When you have an acceptable concept of a belief, you will make no claims as to its finality. To feel that we have arrived is to close the channel for growth. As Harry Emerson Fosdick says to Mr. Brown, "Since when has the Pacific Ocean been poured into a pint tin cup, that the God of this vast universe should be fully comprehended in human words." (1)

Indeed, we must keep our religious concepts subject to repeated, not to say constant, reexamination. Beliefs, at their best, are dynamic and not static. Dan Schneiderman, Mariner IV project director, speaking to Loudon Wainwright, said, "A lot of people got into the act and there was some mind-changing as we went along." He opened the door to a room, and said: "This is where we changed them. We call it the Decision Revision Division." (2) We all need this kind of room where we can make some decision revision. It is as though we were to take a belief from the shelf of our belief library, reexamine it, restate it, and then put it back, saying, "That is what I believe now."

It is not only necessary that we rethink our individual beliefs, such as God, Bible, Jesus, man, the Holy Spirit, and immortality, if we will have a sound faith, but that we consider them as a whole, making sure that they do not contradict each other.

George Orwell describes the world of 1984 as being under

the control of three superstates. Winston Smith, an Outer Party member in the State of Oceania, where "Big Brother" watches over everybody, has a job as a rewrite man in the Ministry of Truth. He makes the state right at all times. He promotes what is known as "doublethink." This does not mean to think twice, but rather "to hold simultaneously two opinions . . . knowing them to be contradictory and believing in both of them. . . ." (3)

We must not let this happen to us in our religious beliefs. We must make sure that what we believe about God is not out of line with what we believe about Jesus and prayer. It is interesting to note that John Calvin began his theological thinking with the assumption that God is sovereign and followed it through logically to predestination. (4) It is rather amazing how many of us have managed to put free will and the all-powerful God together in our thinking. Surely one's belief about man should not make God a tool, or one's view of God make man a puppet, but double thinking permits just this contradiction.

This chapter makes no claim to saying all that could be said about the Christian beliefs. The presentation tries to keep to the fundamentals, leaving it to the reader to give such depth as he may need through other reading.[1]

ABOUT OUR BIBLE

I. *How Were the Books of the Bible Selected?*

The Bible was canonized into its present form at the Council of Carthage in 397 A.D. Those who selected the books that were to make up our Bible were confronted by many choices. It was clear that not all books held sacred by some Christians could, or should, be included. What test must a book pass if it was to be a part of the Bible? Several were tried.

1. THE UNIVERSALLY ACCEPTED TEST (a kind of popularity test) was an early one held by the Christians, but widely differing theological views made this test completely untenable.

2. THE INSPIRATION TEST seemed promising for a time, but so many made claims to being inspired that to use it as a test was to invite disaster.

3. The TEST finally accepted (with a little elasticity and a large chunk of time) was the APOSTOLIC. DID THE MESSENGER OF THE BOOK KNOW JESUS? Did he live in Jesus' time? Paul's writings got in because he claimed (via a vision) to have met Jesus on the Damascus road. Dates and authors were very important under this test, and, without question, some books were accepted that would not have been approved had all the facts been known about one or the other. This is the province of the scholar.

II.   *The Question "How and from Where Did the Messenger Get His Message?"* has never been satisfactorily settled. We are still arguing and debating.

1. An answer that gave the Bible great authority was the DICTATION VIEW. The Bible messenger was a kind of secretary. He took down verbatim what God said. The Bible is *the* word of God. All words in the Bible are of equal value, as are the grains of wheat for making flour. God has said it, and if there is any error, it will be in our interpretation.[2]

   Questioning comment: It would seem reasonable to assume that if an all-powerful, all-knowing God were to turn to the use of language, he surely would have used Jesus to do some writing, not just speaking, leaving to others to recall and write down what he said, who believed one thing about him when they heard him and quite another when they wrote it down.

2. According to the INSPIRATIONAL VIEW, the minds of scriptural messengers were environed by the spirit of God, which so affected what they said as to make their writing the record of a progressive divine revelation, sufficient, when taken together and interpreted by the same spirit who inspired them, to lead every honest inquirer to Christ and salvation.[3]

   Questioning comment: Error of Biblical interpretation will grow out of our failure to bring to the writings the same inspiration as environed the author.

Questioning comment: This would seem to open up the same door for division as appeared when the early church tried to use the inspirational test for selecting the books of the Bible. Why do you need the writings if you have the same spirit as the writer? Why not get it as they got it?

3. THE TESTIMONIAL VIEW of the Bible rests on the proposition that religious truth comes by the examination of the data of experience, which include the five senses plus the sixth. (Note page 70.) Through an intuitive sense, man experiences God, as through his five senses he experiences the physical world about him. From these experiences he comes to certain conclusions and gives testimony to the same. Each of the messengers of the Bible tells us what God meant to him in his time. Each gained from the testimony of those who had gone before and contributed to those who were to follow him.[4]

Supporting comment: This accounts for error in the Bible, even as we find error in all our knowledge, making it clear that if the testimony of the men of yesterday is to be significant, then we must, also, make testimony of what God means to us in our time. We will add to our testimony not only theirs, but the insights that have come to other men since the men of the Bible lived.

Questioning comment: Some will feel that this makes the Bible too much of a human book. It takes the halo from it.

FOUR VIEWS OF GOD

God Is the Name We Give to a Non-thinking, Non-personal Force that stands behind all creation. This "God" does not know that it exists. It is not self-aware. It is neither good nor bad—just a force.

Supporting comment: Nature has no concern for the individual; it is red in tooth and claw. It does, many times, look quite godless.

Questioning comment: This view sidesteps the order that is apparent in the telescopic and microscopic world.

III. God Is the Good and Creative Will of Man

Here we assume, with the materialist, that the universe was a cosmic accident; that man's spiritual stature has come to him via the struggle for existence and the survival of the fittest. Man has so evolved in the flesh that he can now live without the flesh. He has not only become self-aware—he has become eternally so. Man moves out, not just to master the earth where he was created, but he shall strive to master the universe, as he lives beyond the flesh as well as while on earth.[5]

Supporting comment: The greatest argument for this is the greater evidence we have for immortality than we have for God; the fact that this view accepts complete evolution for eternity as well as time. It does not leave us with the question of where God came from. If mind alone can make mind, then who made the first mind, God-mind? What we know about being a person would lead us to believe that it would be impossible to be a person alone, so if we have one God (self-aware being), then we must have many.

Questioning comment: This makes matter and the law of chance the creator. Matter has created thinkers but has no thought behind it. For many, this seems like a vacuum.

IV. God Is the Name One Gives to the Good Will of All Men— Man at His Best

Not only is the Kingdom of God within us, but God is within us. Without us there would be no God.

Supporting comment: This view eliminates the problem of God from man's thinking and makes man, his achievements and aims, all-important on this earth.

Questioning comment: This is strictly a humanistic view, leaving man with no meaning beyond the flesh.

V.   *God Is the Self-Aware Creator of All Things*

He knows that he is, as we know that we are. He is a person
in the highest and noblest sense.[6]

Supporting comment: If the creator of the universe is not
   self-aware, then he is less than you, for you know that
   you are. The universe, say many scientists, looks as though
   it was designed by a designer. Some mathematicians tell
   us that it would be impossible to have created the universe by chance.

1. THE NATURE OF THIS SELF-AWARE GOD

   A. *He is impersonal*; that is, God is self-aware, but only
       remotely aware of what is created. He works accord-
       ing to irrevocable laws. He does not and cannot alter
       them for any reason. Gravity must draw bombs as
       well as bags of food to earth.

Supporting comment: Most of what we see in nature and
   the relationship of God to the events of life would support
   this. A few well-directed tornadoes and lightning bolts,
   sparing the good and striking the evil, would do much to
   undergird many men's confidence in God's presence and
   send men to the peace table.

Questioning comment: This seems to leave out the Father
   God concept taught by Jesus.

   B. *God, all-powerful, either does or permits all that
       occurs in the universe.* He may not do evil, but he
       will, for a good—and many times hidden—purpose
       permit it. God is absolute power, knowledge, pres-
       ence, and perfection. He is the benevolent ruler of the
       universe, always doing what is best.

Supporting comment: This view gives purpose, though hidden, to all that happens in the universe.

Questioning comment: This view seems to take all responsibility from man. He is a kind of robot.

Questioning comment: It makes God, by purpose, responsible
   for *all* the suffering of the universe.

C. *The growing God.* He is tremendously powerful, but not all-powerful. He wills good for all men and is, at all times, doing all that he can for them. The earth is not as good a place as God would have it be for man, nor is it as good as it will some day be, but it is as good as he can make it now. He rejoices in man's joining with him in making this a better world for men, caring for the weak, curing and preventing disease, and ultimately controlling or preventing storms. This God is not only creating but is improving the universe, as we his children do our creating in a much smaller way.[7]

Supporting comment: This view would account for the breakdown in nature on the same basis as man sees his machinery break down; namely, because of mechanical imperfection.

Supporting comment: God simply could not will or permit some things that happen and be good, such as taking parents from their children by death. Or, the killing of twenty thousand-plus people by an earthquake, burying most of them alive.

D. *God is like a parent.* He not only is the creative ruler of the universe, but he gives his personal attention to the needs of the people of earth, as might a king care for some small need of his own child.

Supporting comment: This is what most people would like to think of as being their relationship to God.

Questioning comment: Is it not difficult to make out a case supporting this from what we see happening to people?[8]

FIVE VIEWS OF JESUS

VI. *Jesus Was God*

God came to earth in the person of Jesus and lived, for a time, in the indignities of the flesh and then returned to heaven.

Supporting comment: This is a widely held, historic view
of Jesus.

Questioning comment: Who ran the universe while God was
confined to the flesh?

Questioning comment: If God would do this, could he not
have made the matter clear beyond doubt both by writing
and by demonstration? (Jesus never wrote a line.) Why so
mysterious?

Jesus Was God Incarnate, and when his body died on the cross,
he did not return to heaven but became incarnate in mankind.
God died and made man God. The universe has no God over it,
but man has God immanent.[9]

Supporting comment: If God could lose himself for a time
and become incarnate in one man (Jesus), surely he could
become incarnate in all men and lose himself forever.

Questioning comment: This would seem to impoverish man
rather than enrich him. Does not man need a cosmic
companion—a God that is an "other," quite as much as a
God within?

Jesus Was God's Son by birth (conceived by the Holy Spirit).
At one time he lived with God (in heaven), but by choice
(working it out with God) he came to earth as a man and died
on the cross for the sins of mankind. God, in his perfection,
could not accept sin-soaked (fallen) man without his being
cleaned up, as it were. This required a sacrifice. The Jews had
always used animal sacrifice for this purpose, but God used
Jesus, his son. Jesus paid it all. No more animal sacrifice. What
Jesus did made man acceptable to God for salvation.

Supporting comment: This view of Jesus fits like hand-in-
glove with the Hebrew concept of cleansing man of
sin through the shedding of blood. (Hebrews 9:22) Jesus
was the once-and-for-all sacrifice. The Christian Jews
did not make animal sacrifices for their sins.

Questioning comment: The man who purchased and presented the dove received the benefit of the sacrifice. Who

was to get the benefit of Jesus' sacrifice? Some said the church and its priesthood would determine who was to receive this saving and cleansing power made available through Jesus' death. Others held that man had but to believe that Jesus did it for him and he would have his sin washed away (or forgiven). Is it sensible that God would put Jesus through all this sacrifice and leave this matter so vague for the human race that they could argue and divide over it? Jesus could have written it down so clearly that there would need be no question about it whatsoever, but he did not.[10]

VII. *Jesus Was God's Son, But Not by Necessity—Rather, by Choice*

He was born as all men are born to earth. He chose to give his life to God completely. His untimely death grew out of the vigor with which he pursued this choice. It would have been better for both God and man had he lived longer. He was the finest revelation of what God wants all men to be in their relationship to him, self, others, and conditions about them.[11]

Supporting comment: This view presents Jesus as a real person who, through dedication and prayer, achieved spiritual greatness. He was not an actor. He had to make choices and decisions and take their consequences, as do all men. His faith, like our own, rested mostly on what he believed, not on what he knew. When he said, "Follow me," he had a right to expect it, for he had no advantages closed to others. The significant thing about him was his life—not his death.

Questioning comment: Some will think that this view takes the uniqueness out of Jesus.

Jesus Was Just Another Man Who Caught the Imagination of Men, to Be Compared to Buddha, Mohammed, and Moses

He was not really great, but was made great through the devotion and political ambitions of his followers.

Supporting comment: It is to be recognized that Jesus is not alone among religious leaders who have made claim to a unique relationship to God and have found many followers.

Questioning comment: Many of us see something more in Jesus than a political opportunist a little more clever than some of the other Hebrew prophets.

Two Views of Man

Man Is a Child of the Earth Like the Plant or Animal

H. G. Wells said something like this—many experiences are common to man, but one experience we will never have: we will not know that we are dead. Death is the end of our selfhood as conception is the beginning. At death we are the same as before we were conceived.[12]

Supporting comment: This view is supported by the seeming finality of death and the many characteristics we share with the animal world.

Questioning comment: This, for many, will leave man without purpose.

Man Is a Child of God—Belongs to Eternity, Survives the Flesh

He shall always know that he is. He shall be eternally self-aware.

Supporting comment: The testimony of the sensitives who claim that they have had contact with those who live in the spirit and the fact of Jesus' appearance to his followers after the cross support this view.

Supporting comment: The idea of eternal self-awareness is no more phenomenal than the fact of self-awareness at all. There is one thing man cannot do; he cannot cease to be. Life he will always have. To learn how to live is the end of life. To have eternity on one's hands and not know how to live will be Hell indeed. Heaven is knowing HOW to live with God, self, others, and the situation that confronts us—for time and eternity.[13]

1. THE NATURE OF ETERNAL MAN ON EARTH

   A. *Man is a degenerated child of God.* He is by nature sinful, prone to evil, lost, and unacceptable to his pure and righteous God. He may have, at one time, been perfect, but he did something that robbed him of purity, as mythologically or actually described in the Adam and Eve story. Man was made a little lower than the angels and has been getting a little lower ever since, said Will Rogers.[14]

Supporting comment: That man finds it easy to do evil is beyond dispute. What he would not, that he does.

Questioning comment: If God is all-loving and all-powerful, why did he not make a man that would find it more easy to choose good than evil? This would not make man any less free than now, and possibly more so.

   B. *Man is an immature child of God.* He really is child-like in his growth toward goodness. He has been created by the evolving process, and has come by his body and mind as all creatures of earth have come by their bodies and such mental faculties as they enjoy. The animal drives of the body beset man on every side. They environ his soul and shackle his spirit. He is struggling to move up to godliness and away from animalism. The "prone to evil" is the animal within.[15]

Supporting comment: This view accepts evolution as God's way of creation and recognizes the power of the animal drives in man's life. It has been facetiously said that none of us need to look very far to find a little mule, fox, or skunk in our lives.

2. THE STATE OF ETERNAL MAN AFTER DEATH

   A. *After "death" man fares according to his deeds on earth.* He will, after his physical death, come under the just judgment of God and be assigned to eternal

happiness (heaven, with God) or to eternal damnation (hell, separated from God).

Supporting comment: Much of the church's theology, historically, has supported this view.

Questioning comment: If God is good, how could he permit
such eternal suffering and remain good? If man must
not run out of forgiveness (seventy times seven, said
Jesus), it would seem that God would have to practice
unlimited forgiveness also.

B. *After the death of the flesh, man (if he chooses) may
move on from less to more maturity (Christlike-ness).*
He has within him endless possibilities to grow, as
it were, upward or downward—to have within himself
more and more of heaven or more and more of hell.
Man is always a candidate for good or evil.[16]

Footnote—on God, Jesus, and Man

There are two basic Christian views of the relationship between God, Jesus, and man: one, that they differ in kind, and
the other, that they differ in degree.

They Differ in Kind

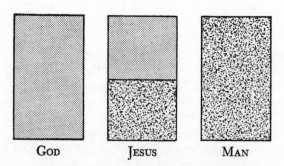

God is divine. Man is human. Jesus is both human and divine.
Or, God is oil; man is water; Jesus is a mixture of the two.

They Differ in Degree

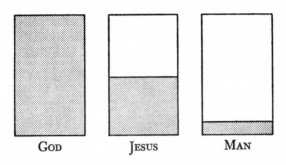

GOD   JESUS   MAN

They are all the same in nature but differ in degree. God is an ocean, Jesus a lake, and man a cup; but they all are filled with water. They differ only in degree, both as to quality and quantity.

If we think of the total divine essence possible as being 100, then God represents, shall we say, 75 percent, Jesus 20 percent, and man 5 percent. The difference would be only in degree. Divine essence is common to them all.[17]

THREE VIEWS OF THE HOLY SPIRIT

A few thoughts in general. Most Christians have a theology concerning the Holy Spirit, but we can concur on only one thing—that it is a mystery. Turn to the Old Testament, and you discover that the Spirit is thought of as something that has its hand in almost everything that happens that is important. The prophets speak of the grass withering because the Spirit of God has blown upon it.

Turn to the New Testament, and you find Jesus trying to describe the Holy Spirit. "The wind bloweth where it listeth and thou hearest the sound thereof, but thou knowest not whence it comes, nor whither it goeth. So is everyone that is born of the Spirit." (John 3:8) John said, "I baptize you with water, but there comes one after me who baptizes with the Holy

Spirit and fire." (Luke 3:15) Notice the comparison: Holy Spirit
and fire. Jesus is said to have asked his followers to tarry until
they were "endued with power from on High." (Luke 24:49)
Pentecost is thought of, by many, to have been that great
moment when the followers of Christ were "set on fire." On
this occasion men were so shaken up that observers mockingly
said they were drunk. What is this power?

The Holy Spirit, as the Ghost of Jesus

Some think of the Holy Spirit as the ghost of Jesus. It is
Jesus come back in person, as he did after the cross, to the men
on the road to Emmaus and the disciples in the upper room,
only we cannot see him, as did they.

  Questioning comment: This was a natural assumption for the
  disciples to make. They had experienced "power" when
  with Jesus in the flesh, and now that he was gone and
  power was still present, they logically concluded it must
  be Jesus come back in spirit—not now confined to some
  place but, in some mysterious way, everywhere.

  Questioning comment: The Apostles' Creed states that Jesus
  was conceived by the Holy Spirit. If accepted, this view
  would be ruled out.

The Holy Spirit as Third Person of the Trinity

Concerning the *Holy Spirit* as the *third person of the Trinity*,
I could do no better than to quote, in part, the Athanasian Creed,
attributed to a Greek bishop (326 A.D.) by the name of Athana-
sius. It was in general use in the West from 850 A.D. and is
retained in the English church service but is omitted from
the American *Book of Common Prayer*. This creed is as follows:

  That we worship one God in Trinity and the Trinity in
  Unity. Neither confusing the Persons, nor dividing the Sub-
  stance. For there is one Person of the Father, another of the
  Son, another of the Holy Ghost, but the Godhead of the
  Father, and of the Son, and of the Holy Ghost is all one. . . .
  The Father infinite, the Son infinite, the Holy Ghost infinite.

The Father eternal, the Son eternal, the Holy Ghost eternal. And yet there are not three eternals, but one eternal. . . . So likewise the Father is almighty, the Son almighty, the Holy Ghost almighty. And yet there are not three almighties, but one almighty. So the Father is God, the Son God, the Holy Ghost God. And yet there are not three Gods, but one God. . . . And in this Trinity there is no before or after, no greater or less. But all three Persons are co-eternal together, and no co-equal. . . . He therefore that would be saved, let him thus think of the Trinity.[18]

Supporting comment: This has been the historic belief of the church with regard to the Holy Spirit.

Questioning comment: Most people of our time find little meaning here.

The Holy Spirit as a Medium of Influence

The Holy Spirit is thought of, by some, as being a *medium of influence*, through which God affects things and people. For instance, I stand before a pulpit and I am aware of the pulpit because of one of my gifts—one of my five senses, the sense of touch. I listen, and I say there is an airplane going over because I hear it. What is the medium by which that plane going over gets down inside me and I know it? We call it "sound." Sound is energy, vibrating at a certain speed. I say there is a picture on the wall. By what medium do I see it? Light—the same substance as sound, only vibrating a little faster. We can become aware of things beyond our five senses through our sixth sense. What medium does one use? Some call it "spirit."[19] Put blinders on a homing pigeon and take him to an unfamiliar place. Let him out, and he goes back home as though you had marked a road map for him. By what medium? Some people call it "nature"; others call it "spirit."

Here is a trumpet vine in the corner of a southern garden, and some twenty-five feet away is a bark-covered pine stump. The vine moves its tentacles this way and that but does not go toward the stump, as it instinctively knows that a bark-covered stump is not a safe support to climb around. And then, one day, the owner of the garden, for decorative purposes, removes the bark from the pine stump, only to find that he has an intruder, for the vine has come, as straight as an arrow, and has wound itself around the stump. By what medium did the trumpet vine know that the bark was, at one time, on and then off the stump? Some call it "nature"; others call it "spirit." When we use this medium between man and man, we call it "telepathy" or "intuitiveness"; but when it is employed in the God-man relationship, we call it "the Holy Spirit."

> *Supporting comment*: This view says simply that God and man employ a commonly used medium in their contact with each other.

> *Questioning comment*: Some will feel that this robs the Holy Spirit concept of its personality.[20]

Five Views of Prayer

Prayer as Nondirective Therapy

Prayer is a nondirective therapy, using God as a counselor. As the one at prayer talks it over, he gets his answer. He talks his way through and out of a problem.

> *Supporting comment*: Prayer may be this and no more, for many of us.

> *Questioning comment*: Most of us are sure that it is more.

Praying to Inform God

Prayer is informing God of what, in the prayer's judgment, God should do.

> *Supporting comment*: Much prayer is of this nature.[21]

> *Questioning comment*: One can hardly imagine anything more presumptuous than an informing prayer.

Praying to Persuade God

Prayer as persuading God assumes that he has everything and that he will give it to us if we can impress upon him our need and worthiness.

Supporting comment: This is an approach to prayer held and practiced by many.

Questioning comment: It seems rather naïve to think of God holding any good back until asked for it. It would be like a parent not getting vitamins for his child because the child did not ask for them.

Prayer as Meeting God's Requirements

God wants me to ask him for things. He could give them without my asking, but, if he did, I would not use them wisely or appreciatively.

Questioning comment: This presupposes that man must know what he needs in order to get the most from God. In the meantime, God holds it in storage—one instinctively feels that this cannot be true.

Prayer as Faithing with God

God creates by faith, and we create by Faith. (Page 51.) When we use our faith with God and not against him, that is prayer.[22]

Supporting comment: It also includes our focusing the creative energy of God through our faith on the situation of our concern, as a magnifying lens concentrates the rays of the sun. (Page 52.)

Supporting comment: This view makes prayer an act of creative importance and does not present us with a God who chooses between his children.

Supporting comment: This gives man a responsibility and maturing relationship with God.

Questioning comment: It does not make God the single source of spiritual power.

THREE VIEWS OF GRACE

Grace as Unmerited Favor

Grace, in Christian tradition, has been thought of as an unmerited favor that God has bestowed upon mankind. Man merits eternal damnation, but God is doing all he can to save him.

> *Questioning comment*: This view has hardly seemed worthy of a loving God. Love *has* to do all it can. Since God made man, how can he do less than *all* to help him? If man is a child of God, he merits all that both God and man can do to make him equal to his position.

Grace as Divine Influence Acting on Man

Grace is thought of as a divine influence acting on man—a spiritual leavening force. As we are affected by the love of another, so God (and Jesus) affect us. God is to us as the sun is to a plant, stirring us to life.

Grace as Available Power

Grace is also thought of as being the name we give to a power that is available to us. We may think of this power as: (a) a radiance from God, a creative love light; (b) the creative spiritual energy of the universe which both God and man use when they faith. It is a source of power which is available to us and may be tapped by faith.[23]

> *Supporting comment*: Surely there is a spiritual force that is available to us at all times, whatever we call it or claim its source to be. As the seed will not be helped by the sun that shines on the dark, sealed box in which it is imprisoned, neither will this spiritual radiance help us unless we let it in. God does not hold (nor has he ever held) anything back from man. It is man that holds him back.

Two Kinds of Evil

Natural Evil

When we define natural evil, we think of those forces of nature (tornadoes, earthquakes, lightning, floods, drought, disease, and so forth) which threaten or destroy the creative comforts and security of man and over which he has little or no control, described by some as "acts of God."

1. SOURCES OF NATURAL EVIL

    A. *Natural evil is natural.* Some say that natural evil is really *not evil at all.* Nature propagates by the survival of the fittest, and this competitiveness must extend to the whole of nature. There is no way for God, even if he would, to exclude the body of man from it. Disease germs and lightning are as much a part of nature as trees and grass.

Supporting comment: Nature is certainly red with tooth and claw. Only man cares for the individual. Nature is interested only in the survival of the species. The weak are the food for the strong.

Questioning comment: This is a cold way of seeing life and seems to leave something out. Jesus taught his followers to care for the weak, and that he came to seek and to save the lost.

    B. *God's way of testing or punishing men.* There are those who believe (at least, they say they do) that God causes, or permits, either the devil or nature to do all evil; he could, and does, alter the course of nature at any point where he may choose. The answer to the question, "What have I done that this should happen to me?" is that God has a purpose, and you will see. Maybe you have done, or are about to do, evil, and he wants to correct you—to get you or keep you on course, or, even more important, God may need you for some great service in the future, and he is giving you this trial to give you strength.

Questioning comment: This just does not seem to work out in experience. We have all seen too many lives ruined by the loss of parents through untimely deaths due to natural causes, to mention just one instance.

    C. *Natural evil is the breaking down of the cosmic machine.* Many see more in natural evil than the side effects of the struggle for existence, though they

do see this. They also see the manifestation of the
breakdown of a great machine. This world of ours
(make it as small or as large as you will) is highly
engineered. The parts do not always run smoothly.
They get out of line. Cell multiplication is necessary
for the creating and sustaining of life, but when the
process breaks down and goes wild, we have cancer.
We would smother for oxygen if air should stop cir-
culating (cold air coming down, hot air going up),
but when this process goes wild, we have hurricanes
and tornadoes.[24]

Supporting comment: This view parallels man's creative experience in making machines. We seem never to have
made machines so perfect that none will break down.

Supporting comment: This view would call the destructive-
ness of nature to the creature security of man an evil
neither planned nor wanted by God, but rather an expression of the imperfection of the natural order as related to man—a self-aware being.

Supporting comment: This would make man's efforts to correct nature a labor of assistance, helping God to make
this a better place to live for a child of God. Is not this
breakdown in nature evidence that we have a creating
as well as a creator God; a God who grows and learns
from experience, as mind at its best must always do?[25]

Moral Evil

By "moral evil" we mean those acts or attitudes (sex, lying,
stealing, deceiving, injuring, killing, and so forth) which debase
the doer or injure another, physically or spiritually.

1. THREE SOURCES OF MORAL EVIL

A. *Innate evil nature of man*. Moral evil has, for centuries, been attributed to the innate evil nature of
man (in Adam all sinned), but, whatever its source,
we have inherited an evil tendency that is reflected
in all that we do. We are prone to evil. It is from

this moral depravity that man must be rescued, because God gave man freedom, and he has abused it.

Supporting comment: This has been the traditional message of the church through the years.

Questioning comment: For many it has seemed impossible to fit this concept of evil into the idea of God as a Father.

B. *The conflict between spiritual values and animal drives.* Moral evil certainly has some relationship to our bodies. We do live in the same kind of bodies as the animals about us—bodies in which survival is the first law of life. We all know the power of environment over the spirit of man.

C. *Man's negative use of creative power.* Man has creative power as does God, and when he uses it against God, that is evil[26] Man's closest physical environment is this animal body, with its drives and instincts.

Supporting comment: Moral evil would result when man failed to handle, in a Christian way, these drives he has inherited from his animal past.

Suporting comment: Man does evil not because he is prone to do wrong, but because he is an immature child of God. He is not spiritually big enough to avoid making poor choices and yielding to the pressures of his physical and spiritual drives.

A PERSONAL NOTE

I wish I could speak with you personally at this point in our journey. Remember, you do not have to take any particular viewpoint. No one is trying to force anything upon you. If past experience is any guide to our present, I am sure you may well feel the need for much more thinking and rethinking. I hope you will! My only prayer is that you will continue to wrestle with these beliefs until you can say, of an increasing number of them, "This is what I believe now"—keeping constantly in mind that faith (a feeling the opposite of fear, and which is the vital force of the Christian religion) is rooted in belief; that your faith is rooted, not in what the church or someone else believes, but in what *you believe.*

All too often, all too many of us are pathetically trying to hold fast to a faith in something that reason has long since discarded, little realizing that we are trying to do the impossible. When our beliefs become intellectually indefensible, our faith, like a cut flower, soon withers.

NOTES

1. Bishop Gerald Kennedy's "I Believe" will be helpful to many.
2. Restate this view. What has been its greatest weakness and strength? Are there many who hold it now?
3. What do you consider to be the strength and weakness of this view?
4. What are the weaknesses and strength of this view? Does it, in your mind, add to or subtract from the importance of the Bible in our space age?
5. If you want to do some close thinking, read some of Paul Tillich and Bishop Robinson with this view in mind.

Do you think that is what they believe?

What do you like and dislike about it?
6. What percentage of the Christians you know do you think hold this view of God?
7. Compare faith and evil. (Page 55.)
8. What is your reaction to this comment?
9. Compare the "God is dead" movement.
10. What other supporting or questioning comment can you add to these? If you know a clergyman that holds this view, why not arrange an interview?
11. What other supporting and questioning comments can you add to this?
12. Why not interview someone who holds this view? Do not argue—just note his answers to your questions. A tape recorder is helpful for this.
13. Restate this view. Find a clergyman and ask him to share with you his belief in the hereafter. Does this make "heaven" and "hell" places or attitudes?
14. What other supporting and questioning comments can you add to these?
15. What other supporting and questioning comments can you add to these?
16. Compare this with the creative view of prayer—page 52.

17. Which of these two views do you like the most and why? Would you like to add or subtract anything?

18. Try to restate this view in non theological language.

19. Turn again to page 70; here we discuss the place of the sixth sense in gaining spiritual truth.

20. What view of the Holy Spirit do you like best and why?

21. Study your own prayers at this point.

22. What is your understanding of this statement?

23. Compare page 90 ff. What does the Grace of God mean to you?

24. Compare growing God concept on page 79.

25. Restate this.

26. Review pages 91-93 and restate this view of evil. State both a questioning and a supporting comment.

CHAPTER VII

Creating the Belief and Faith Self-Image

OUR QUEST: *To find how the belief self-image is created from our beliefs, and how it, in turn, is changed into a faith (feeling) self-image.*

The Belief Self-Image

The B.S.I. is what we believe about ourselves because of what we believe about many other things—including God. It is the belief through which all our other beliefs become effective in our lives. As a group of leaders may elect someone to lead them and direct their services, so do all the other beliefs in our lives work through the B.S.I.

A diagram may help:

BELIEFS

Religious			General
1—God	☒	◼	Ability—13
2—Jesus	☐	☐	Education—14
3—Bible	☐	☐	Position—15
4—Holy Spirit	☐	☐	Appearance—16
5—Prayer	☒	☐	Handicap—17
6—Faith	☒	YOUR BELIEF SELF-IMAGE	☐	Money—18
7—Immortality	☐		☐	Clothes—19
8—Man	☐	Because of my belief about "X" and "O"	☐	Experience—20
9—Church	☐		☐	failure—a
10—Evil	☐	I believe that in my relationship	☐	success—b
11—Intuitive			☐	Health—21
awareness	☐	to	☐	Personality—22
12—Charms	☐		☐	Family—23
		I can be	◼	Example—24

It may read something like this: "Because of what I believe about 'X' and 'O,' I believe that, in my relationship to 'a certain problem or person in my life,' I can succeed."[1]

Each belief will affect the B.S.I. in ratio to the depth with which it is held. If our negative beliefs are held with more depth than our positive ones, we will have a negative B.S.I. Sometimes our B.S.I. is controlled almost completely by one great, all-possessing belief, so that one can hardly distinguish between the B.S.I. and the belief itself. For instance, Mary Bethune said, "I believe in God so I believe in Mary Bethune." George Whitefield makes it quite clear that God was central in what he believed about himself in a difficult situation. "George Whitefield," says Bishop Hazen Werner, "gives in his journal an account of his experiences on the ocean during his journey to America in 1738. In those days travel was precarious and difficult; months were consumed in a journey of that kind. In this particular instance, Whitefield was faced with the likelihood of an impending disaster. He writes in his journal, 'Our allowance of water is just one pint a day; our sails are exceedingly thin and some of them last night were split and no one knows where we are. But . . . God does and that is sufficient.'" (1) He believed that, in his situation, all things would work out for good because of what he believed about God.

Sir Wilfred Grenfell tells of a deeply religious woman in Labrador who fell on the ice and crushed her leg. Infection set in and, to save her life, they had to amputate. She believed that it was clearly stated in the Bible that God wanted his children to bear the pain that he sent to them, so she refused to take an anesthetic. Her five grown sons held her down while Doctor Grenfell cut off the leg. She never whimpered. She had a belief self-image that was all but completely shaped by a personal belief about the Bible and God.

To move from one extreme to another, many who call themselves Christian would be surprised to find how few of their Christian beliefs are used in forming their B.S.I.; they do not realize they are making so small a use of the great Christian insights in their daily living.

Dr. Maxwell Maltz, in his practice as a plastic surgeon, found that when he changed a person's appearance, he often changed his character. Why? Because he had changed this person's B.S.I.

He discovered that, whereas before the plastic surgery, the patient may have said within herself, "In my relationship to life I am a failure because of my appearance." After the operation she would say, "I am a success because I am attractive and wanted."[2] (2)

I daresay that many of Doctor Maltz's patients were Christians but little realized how much of what they believed about their nose, and how little of what they believed about God, went into the making of their B.S.I.[3] Take the case of Mrs. Miriam Eubanks of Syracuse, New York, who was apprehended and imprisoned for cashing bad checks. At one time she had been a respected woman in her community. When asked why she suffered such character deterioration, she pinpointed two things: first, the event of her son being born physically and mentally handicapped, and second, the occasion when she found that she was an adopted child. It would be my guess that she was a religious person but her B.S.I. was supported entirely by her belief in the nobility of her family origin. When that was gone, she had no other belief to which she could turn. Her B.S.I. collapsed and took her faith with it.

No matter how much we dress up the process by psychological or theological language, this is where character and personality change always begins—in the creation of a belief self-image from religious and general beliefs.

The best belief self-image will always rest on a wide belief base. The spare tire is of no real need until we get a puncture—and one may rest his B.S.I. on a single belief as long as it is not threatened. It is rather pathetic to see someone frantically holding onto some belief, like a drowning man to straw, because he has built the entire superstructure of his spiritual life upon it. I had a woman in one of my classes who was so threatened by my presentation of different views of the Bible that she labeled me as "unchristian" and left the church. She really was a fine person, but her B.S.I. rested on too narrow a belief base for the rigors of "truth pursuing" as over against "truth defending."

In the remainder of this chapter we are to give special attention to the Faith Self-Image (Fa.S.I.)—HOW we move from believing to feeling. We know that beliefs and the B.S.I. come from reason, but from where do we get faith—the feeling side of religion and life?

The Faith Self-Image

On the inside cover of a popular magazine was the picture of a child trying to put pegs and holes together. There was evidence of both success and failure. The caption under the picture read: "From Experience Comes Faith." And so it does!

Would you have faith? Then, go *do—live—practice* what you believe (intellectually accepted as true), until you *feel* it as true. Only from experience comes faith. John Wesley became persuaded that the Moravian religion experience was what he wanted and asked their leader, Peter Boehlor, "How can I get it?" Boehlor's now famous reply was, "Practice it until you get it."

From experience come both faith and fear. Success experience gives us faith; failure experience gives us fear. We are all replete with illustrations of this from our own experiences of walking, skating, speaking, riding a bicycle, driving a car, and, for some, piloting a plane. In each case, the more success experience we have, the greater becomes our faith. The more failure experience we have, the greater becomes our fear. Though it is clear that both faith and fear come from experience, what we must not overlook is that there are two kinds of experience—two ways of doing—*actual* and *imaginative*.

Actual Experience

A Sunday newspaper supplement carried the story of Carol Nelson, a sky-diver. On May 30, 1960, her mother and father were at Elsinore, California, to watch her dive. She tells of circling in the plane at 25,000 feet and seeing the drop zone. She jumped at the proper time, but instead of falling clear, she dangled by one of her chute ropes from the oil-streaked belly of the ship, gliding through the sky like a water-skier, directly behind the deadly, flashing propeller blades. She did not dare let out the chute. If she did, it would have stalled the plane and all would have crashed. So Carlos, the one who was managing her jump from the plane, took a knife and cut the rope. Before he cut it, Carol patted her reserve chute, thinking to herself how glad she was to have it—her only hope.

As she plunged toward the earth, she pulled the ripcord of the second chute, but it did not open, and the ground seemed to be rushing up to meet her. She then realized that she was falling upside down and, thus, the wind was holding the chute closed. "I moved my arms and rolled over," she said, "then dug my fingers deep into the pack and dragged out the silk, throwing it to the wind. There was a comforting yank. The parachute blossomed. I was floating gently earthward."

Carol made a perfect landing, and as she sat there feeling the earth, letting the sand run through her fingers, a jeep raced up and skidded to a stop.

"Are you O.K.?" the driver yelled.

"I nodded, and then saw Mother sitting beside him. I could tell she was fighting back tears. When I climbed in, she hugged me, and then said sternly, 'Carol, your father and I want you to go right up and jump again.'" (3) Why? Of all things! Because from experience comes faith and fear, and they wanted her latest actual experience to be faith—, not fear-creating. Had she not jumped for another month, she may well have lost the faith necessary to perform the art—which leads us to examine the second type of faith-creating experience.

Imaginative Experience

Carol had a positive B.S.I. concerning sky-diving (we do not know how much of her belief in God, in prayer, in her trainer, and in past success had each contributed to it), and the more times she successfully dove, actually or imaginatively, the more her B.S.I. became a Fa.S.I.[4]

But let us suppose Carol's positive B.S.I. rested mostly on her past success, and the second chute had only partly opened, saving her from death but leaving her with a broken vertebra; that to mend her back, she had to lie flat for several months. She would have begun her convalescence with a negative B.S.I. created by a near-failure, and, let us suppose, as she lies in the hospital, she dreams and imagines herself in terms of it until she becomes fearful and decides to stop diving. It is clear to see that it was not the *actual* but the imaginative experience that made her fear-filled and led to her decision. Indeed, though most of our fearing and faithing have their beginning in actual experience, it is imaginative experience that gives them depth and force.[5]

Reverend Clayton Williams, former minister of the American Church in Paris, France, tells of an incident which supports this observation. It seems that a Russian railroad employee entered a refrigerator car only to have the door close and lock behind him. He could find no way to escape, nor could he attract anyone's attention to his plight.

Finally, the worker resigned himself to his fate. He left a record of his slow demise on the wall of the car, where he wrote, "I am becoming cold." A little later he wrote, "Still colder now." Under that, "Nothing to do but wait." A little later he feebly wrote, "I am slowly freezing to death. I am half asleep now. I can hardly write." Then finally, "These are my last words." And they were.

When the car was opened and the body found, the temperature was only fifty-six degrees. The worker had never been colder than that—for the freezing mechanism of the car had long since been out of order. There was also plenty of air in the car. This man had *not actually* frozen or smothered to death. He had been killed by fear, and all the fear-creating experience had been imaginative. Finding no means of escape, he had constructed a negative B.S.I. (a false one), which was accepted by him as true—and then gave it such depth, through his imaginative practice, as to produce a death-dealing fear.[6]

Jackie Jensen, Boston Red Sox outfielder, had an airplane phobia. He was afraid to ride in planes. A U.P. writer says that this fear of riding in planes originated in a childhood experience of seeing a model airplane crash. Certainly, the actual experience could hardly have been of less significance, but his repeated imaginative experiences created a deep-seated and mastering fear.

Mrs. Gormel and her husband, while out for a ride, stopped to change drivers and were back on the road moving at some five miles an hour when a speeding automobile, moving in the same direction, struck the rear of their car. It was a terrific crash, and both Mr. and Mrs. Gormel found themselves piled up in what was left of the back seat. No bones were broken and bruises were surprisingly few for such an accident.

When I, as their pastor, called, Mrs. Gormel related the details of the crash to me at great length. I sat out the coming and going of several neighbors and friends, listening while she repeatedly and vividly reviewed her accident experience—the crash, the silence, the pain, the dark. When the last guest had gone, she turned to me and said, "You know, pastor, I've been told that I'll be fortunate if I don't have a nervous breakdown because of this accident."

I tried as best as I could to make Mrs. Gormel see that, although she had withstood the actual experience of the accident quite well, it was the repeated imaginative experience that could give her a nervous breakdown. I placed my finger on the arm of the chair and hit it a rather stern blow with the side of my fist. Speaking to her, I said, "That didn't hurt me much, but if I were to hit my finger in this same manner over and over again for one hundred times, the pain would be excruciating. So it is, Mrs. Gormel, with your nerves, if you repeat this accident experience hundreds of times imaginatively, ultimately they will become so sick that they will break down. You must stop 'having the accident' or you *will* have a nervous breakdown." To experience anything imaginatively is to experience it—and from experience comes both fear and faith.[7]

The need for imaginative control. If we would eliminate fear and establish faith as the dominant force in our lives, it is obvious that we must find a way to control the imagination—a way to keep our imaginative experience faith- rather than fear-creating. The pessimist has an imagination that has been conditioned to the visualization of negative B.S.I. In any given situation he always imagines the worst happening to him. He lives constantly in the substance of the things he does not want. His imagination is completely out of control. The optimist, by contrast, has an imagination conditioned by visualizing the positive possibilities, thereby keeping his life faith-centered. He gets the substance of the things hoped for.

One day, while doing pastoral calling in a stick-shift automobile, I drew up to the curb, parking close behind another car. When I was ready to leave, it was necessary to put my car into reverse in order to draw away from the one in front of me. This I did, but, to my dismay, when I was ready to go forward again, I could not shift gears. They were stuck in reverse. The engine was working splendidly, generating plenty of power to draw my car at high speed down the street or the highway to my next call, but I could use that power in only one way—to go backwards.

I backed down the street (it seems down when you are going backwards) into a garage. They were busy and could not help me for an hour or more, so I backed through the garage, out another door, and onto the street, going in the right direction but going backwards. Before I found a garage to work on my car, the radiator was boiling.

As the reverse gear of a car should serve only to get us out (or keep us out) of tight places, so should fear serve only as a short-term, or emergency, emotion. It should never be used as a way of life. A fear-ridden person has an imagination stuck in reverse.

May I first illustrate and then diagram this need of controlling imaginative experience? Mrs. A. and Mrs. B. are sitting together in the back seat of a car, taking a Sunday afternoon pleasure trip. The same possibilities for happiness and for accident exist for them both, but how differently they react to the same experience! Mrs. A. had a wonderful and exhilarating time during the entire ride. She arrived home "fit as a fiddle" and very relaxed. Mrs. B., on the other hand, arrived home as taut as a fiddle string and completely unnerved. The difference between the two is clearly a matter of imaginative control. Mrs. A. visualized the ride in terms of its good and Mrs. B in terms of its bad possibilities. We repeat, it is the B.S.I. which most successfully holds the imagination captive that exerts the most power over our lives. One may have the best possibilities in the world, but at the same time live an emotionally defeated life IF his imagination is used only to visualize himself in terms of his negative ones.[8] As further illustration, take the matter of "walking a plank."

To imagine oneself walking the plank (A) is to have the experience of walking it, and from this imaginative experience comes faith. To imagine oneself falling off the plank (B) is to have the experience of falling off, and from this experience comes fear. The successful person will choose the faith-, rather than the fear-producing imaginative experience.[9]

We have many illustrations of the part that the control of our imaginative experience plays in our achievements and failures at golf.

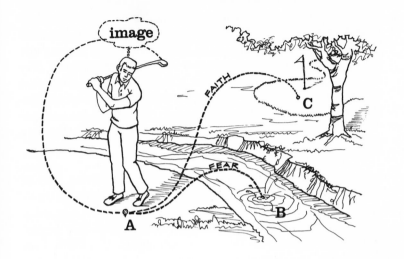

In the above picture there is a stream of water (B) between the tee (A) on the mound and the distant green (C). If, as the golfer stands there, he imagines himself hitting the ball and its going into the water, then he has had the kind of imaginative experience that produces fear, especially if he has a new ball. If, on the other hand, he has imagined his ball as moving straight out over the stream and onto the green, he has had faith-creating imaginative experience.

The trapeze artist has long since learned that he must "throw his heart" over the bar first, and any good pinch hitter must have done a lot of hitting before the pinch, and most of it will have been imaginative.

This need of selecting our imaginative experience may be diagrammed in a number of different ways.

In the "imaginative control chart," page 106, the solid lines represent the areas of positive B.S.I.; the broken lines, the areas of negative B.S.I. Each line might represent an average day of fearing and faithing—the time spent in visualizing one's life in terms of positive and negative beliefs. (0) at the bottom of the chart would represent a day in which one's imagination was

used completely in the area of negative B.S.I.; whereas (10) at the top of the chart would represent a day in which one's imagination was used completely in the areas of positive B.S.I. The question of first importance, as one searches for mental health through faith, is: How does one increase his control over his imaginative experience, moving the faith-fear line from (0) to (10)?[10]

The following may serve as a kind of summary diagram on the need for selectivity in imaginative experience.

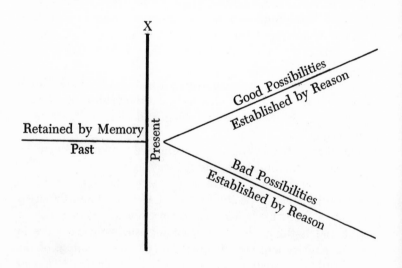

Standing on the line marked "Present" at the point X, memory tells me what has happened, both good and bad. Reason tells me what could happen, both good and bad. Imagination says, "Look; it's happening now." Happiness today does not depend primarily upon what experience memory tells me I *have* had, or what experience reason tells me I *may* have, but which of these past, or possible, experiences is imaginatively being experienced now. The imagination out of control may be likened to the fire burning down your house, but, when under control, to the fire in the furnace which keeps the house warm on a cold winter night, giving comfort to all.[11]

NOTES

1. Can one's view of God create a negative B.S.I.? How?

2. This is not a religious-centered book, but is rewarding reading for those who would like to pursue the B.S.I. concept with greater depth.

3. How much of the average Christian's B.S.I. is based on general belief and facts as presented in the chart on page 96, and how much on religious beliefs?

4. Note several possible compositions for Carol's B.S.I. prior to her jump, using the chart on page 106.

5. How often have you experienced this in your own life? A case or two would be helpful.

6. Some might like to call this "negative-faithing" rather than "fearing." What do you think?

7. Will a member of the group state what is meant here by "actual" and "imaginative" experience? Draw on your own experiences to illustrate both.

8. Do you know of anyone who lives in terms of their negative beliefs? Illustrate.

9. Have you ever found yourself doing this when confronted by a difficult task?

10. Between 0 and 10, which number would seem to be a normal way to faith and fear?

11. Discuss this statement: "We all have both negative and positive B.S.I.'s. It is through imaginative control that we determine which of them shall be emotionalized and become our feeling self-image."

CHAPTER VIII

Achieving Faith-Creating
Imaginative Experience

OUR QUEST: *To observe how the spiritually successful keep the creative imagination under control and thus create faith through the deliberate and intellectual use of imagination as well as actual experience.*

In the creating of imaginative experience, there are three basic methods that we use in one way or another to shift the imagination from one belief (B.S.I.) to another. They are diversion, reason, and suggestion.

DIVERSION

"John," says the physician, "you are all run down (meaning, of course, that he is all wound up). You must get away for a while. Why don't you take your wife and go away for a holiday?"

"Getting away" has perfected many a cure because it is one way of effectively breaking the grip of a negative B.S.I. on the imagination, moving the imagination (*B*), as in the illustration on the next page, from the *C* to the *A* position.

The imagination cannot be in two places at the same time. For many people the pursuit of creative hobbies will serve to divert their imagination; that is, diversion will get the imagination to move from the negative to the positive B.S.I. Somewhere I read of a father who went golfing and upon his return asked his wife what their son, Harry, had been doing all morning. "Why, John!" she exclaimed, horrified, "he was caddying for you!" The father, still thinking about his game, mumbled, "I thought that caddy looked familiar."

Though this may be overdoing it a bit, his mind was, for sure, on his game. L. W.'s self-image in his work is one of failure, but on the golf course, where he repeatedly makes a par, he feels successful, and since faith comes from experience, a few hours on the golf course has set L. W. back in business again. He's a new man.

Any kind of community service may have real diversional value to folks who develop "ingrown eyeballs," as a friend of mine calls them. Such work will be fraught with certain disappointments and failures, but, at least, it will divert the imagination from the self to social or organizational problems.

The above is reminiscent of the man who enjoyed the reputation of knowing how to manage mules, no matter how balky. When asked to share his secret of success, he said, "Well, sir, when I'm plowing and the mule stops, I just pick up some soil, put it in his mouth to taste, then he goes right along."

"Why do you think the dirt affects him that way?" he was asked.

"Well, sir, I really don't know, but I think it makes him forget what he was thinking about."

This method works for human beings quite as well as for

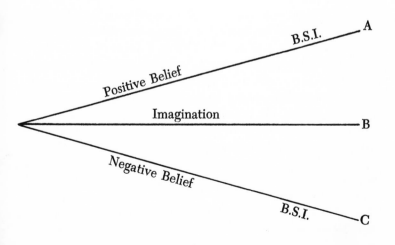

mules. A person who stutters in ordinary conversation, many times, talks fluently when angry. The "dirt in his mouth" diverts his attention from speech to something else. Carlyle looked upon work as "the grand cure for all maladies and miseries that ever beset mankind." It does seem, at times, that the happiest people are those who are too busy to be unhappy.[1]

If the imagination could always be shifted from the negative to the positive B.S.I. by diversion, life would be simple indeed, but all too often our negative B.S.I. has such a grip on our imagination that diversion is not strong enough to break it away.

Several years ago, upon returning from my vacation rested and filled with zeal for my job, I met a man of our village who had also just returned from his. We exchanged the ordinary greetings, and I remarked that I had had a grand time while away but that I was glad to be back. I shall never forget the look on his face when he said, "I wish I could have stayed away." Within two weeks he was confined to his bed, and within a month his business had failed. What he was trying to tell me, in our brief conversation, was that he had never been away. His efforts to use diversion had failed completely.

The second way by which we may shift the imagination from one B.S.I. to another is—*reason*.

REASON

Reason plays two parts in imaginative control. First, it explains away negative beliefs that support our negative B.S.I. Second, it establishes and undergirds positive ones. You will want to familiarize yourself with the diagram on the opposite page.

The pendulum of Mr. Hepmann's imagination had been held fast by a negative belief (C) concerning his own health. He had believed that his heart was on its "last legs." He had gone to his physician, who, after due examination, explained to him that what he, Mr. Hepmann, thought was heart trouble was really a flare-up of his gall bladder, causing indigestion. This explanation dissolved Mr. Hepmann's negative belief (C) that his heart was damaged and substituted a positive belief (A)

that his physical condition was not serious. The physician gave him some pills which he said would correct the situation and told Mr. Hepmann that he would be well in a few days—and he was! Not only did the pills help him, but his imagination, free from his negative belief, dissolved by the doctor's reasoning about his heart, was permitted to swing back to positive beliefs about the business of living.[2]

Mrs. Layworth is awakened in the wee hours of the morning by a noise in the attic. In fact, the more she thinks about it, the more clearly she can hear footsteps! A negative belief (*C*) has taken her imagination captive. It is intensified by recalling that when she returned from her club meeting late in the afternoon, she had sensed that a living room chair was not at its usual angle and that the window near it was unlocked.

Now thoroughly frightened, Mrs. Layworth awakens her husband, and they listen together. She urges him to investigate. He can hardly refuse and retain his masculine integrity, so Mr. Layworth, flashlight in hand, repairs to the attic and shoots the light about.

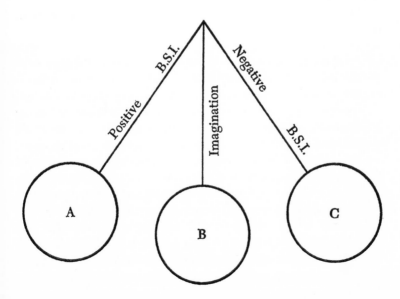

Instead of an intruder, Mr. Layworth finds an attic window down from the top a bit to ensure ventilation, allowing the wind to blow the window shade gently back and forth. He is sure he has found the source of the noise and, returning to his room, explains it to his wife. In minutes they are both sound asleep. Reason has dissolved their negative belief (C) (someone in the attic), thereby freeing their imaginations to swing back to the positive belief (A) that all is well in their house.

Now, the next morning, Mr. Layworth goes to the attic to get some money which they had secretly stored there and, to his horror, he finds that it is gone. It is evident that they *had* heard someone in the attic during the night, and that the intruder had been hiding behind the chimney that ran up through the corner of the attic at the time Mr. Layworth had made his "investigation."

What we want to observe here is that the Layworth's faith rested on a positive belief which reason had falsely given them, but, since it was true to the Layworths, it gave them faith. It is important for us to see that, though we may get faith from false beliefs, the belief must be true for us.[3]

Dr. Alfred Adler used reason to dissolve a negative belief in his practice of psychiatry.

A certain thirty-year-old man of extraordinarily aggressive character, who achieved success and honor despite difficulties in his development, comes to the physician in circumstances of greatest depression and complains that he has no desire to work or to live. He explains that he is about to be engaged, but that he looks at the future with great mistrust. He is plagued by a strong jealousy, and there is great danger that his engagement will be broken. The facts in the case, which he brings up to prove his point, are not very convincing. Since no one can reproach the young lady, the obvious distrust which he shows lays him open to suspicion. He is one of those many men who approach another individual, feel themselves attracted but immediately assume an aggressive attitude which destroys the very contact which they seek to establish.

Now let us plot the graph of this man's style of life as we have indicated above, by taking out one event in his life and seeking to join it with his present attitude. According to our experience, we usually demand the first childhood remembrance, even though we know it is not always possible to test the value of this remembrance objectively. This was his first childhood remembrance—he was at the marketplace with his mother and younger brother. Because of the turmoil and crowding, his mother took him, the elder brother, on her arm. As she noticed her error, she put him down again and took the younger child up, leaving our patient to run around, crushed by the crowd, very much perplexed. At that time he was four years old. In the recital of this remembrance, we hear the identical notes that we surmised in a description of his present complaint. He is not certain of being the favored one, and he cannot bear to think that another might be favored. Once the connection is made clear to him, our patient, very much astonished, sees the relationship immediately. (1)

This man was visualizing himself in terms of some negative beliefs. (B.S.I.) Under Doctor Adler's guidance, he came to see that the cause of his trouble was of little consequence. His negative belief was dissolved and he was free to visualize his life in terms of his positive belief about his sweetheart. There is little question but that reason played a major part in shifting this man's imagination from a negative to a positive belief—from fear to faith.

In all truth, one should say that the success a therapist may have in using reason to dissolve negative beliefs, which hold the imagination captive, is not always due to his ability to discover the exact cause of the person's trouble, but rather to the fact that the explanation which he gives, or that the patient discovers, is intellectually acceptable to him.[4]

We recall the stand of the Greeks against the King of Persia at Salamis Bay. The Greeks abandoned their country, and the women, old people, and children made camp on the rocky island of Salamis. All the able-bodied men manned their boats, their "wooden walls," as they put it—the Athenian fleet. The Greeks bet everything they had on the fleet, outnumbered by the Persians three to one.

To the Persians, the mastering of the Athenian fleet was all-important, for without it they could not support their army so far from home base. King Xerxes of Persia enthroned himself on a high headland to watch his huge armada triumph, but instead looked on in anguish while his ships were routed or destroyed. The Greeks, who had staked all on their ships, had won.

Why did the Greeks have such faith in the "wooden walls" when they were outnumbered three to one? The answer is that the Oracle had said they *would* win, and, since they believed in the Oracle, they gained faith and saved the day. The pronouncements or oracles would do little or nothing for us because we do not believe in them. It would not be reasonable. But for those who did believe in them, they made the difference between faith and fear—success and failure.

In one sequence of Charles M. Schulz' series, "Peanuts," Charlie Brown and Lucy are watching a torrential rain through the window. She says, "Boy, look at it rain! What if it floods the whole world?"

He replied, "It will never do that. In the ninth chapter of Genesis God promised Noah that it would never happen again, and the sign of the promise is the rainbow."

Lucy sighs, "You've taken a great load off my mind."

"Sound theology has a way of doing that," Charlie Brown answers pontifically.

Even an unsound theology may take a load off the mind of the believer.

Parenthetically, and before we leave our consideration of the place of reason in imaginative control, we should correct any impression that it does not make any difference what we believe. It certainly does! The more shallow and untested the belief, the more easily it can be washed out and undermine the faith that rests upon it. We have all seen this happen.

Bishop Ensley writes, "I recall a small-town piano teacher in his mid-fifties who suddenly decided that he should enter upon a concert career. He pulled up stakes, sold his goods, cut his ties with his security and moved to a distant city to become a piano virtuoso. Needless to say, his failure was complete. There was nothing intrinsically wrong with the ideal; to be an artist of the piano is most admirable. But the reality of the situation—the want of ability and the time of life—defeated him. How much mischief in life is caused by the exaltation of ideals that are discordant with reality!" (2) We may add, how much mischief in life is caused by grounding our faith on beliefs that are discordant with reality! One can build his house (faith) on the sand (false or weak belief), but it will have a precarious future.

SUGGESTION

Of the three ways used to achieve faith-creating imaginative experience—diversion, reason, and suggestion—it is probably the last that is the most important. Suggestion falls into one of four basic categories: *charms, example, association,* and *affirmation.*

Charms

Charms are a widely used method of creating imaginative experience. By "charms" we mean anything that is believed to have magical power over the possessor's life. A charm may take on one of a number of possible forms.

During World War II, my brother Rex served for some time in the South Sea islands. In one letter he described how the natives used charms to create faith. "They have pieces of colored cloth strung up on high bamboo poles outside of their huts which they believe will keep evil spirits away." Certainly, they did keep much evil away, for because of them the natives had faith; without these bits of cloths they would have had fear, which will make anyone not only a candidate but, what is more, a magnet for trouble. We must not be misled into thinking that backward peoples have a monopoly on the use of charms. Most of us have something or other in our lives which gives us positive, faith-creating, imaginative experience. We also have our de-charms, which we avoid like a plague. Not many people want to walk under a ladder or have a black cat cross the road in front of them. Neither do they want to attempt some great feat on Friday the thirteenth, because it makes them feel like subjects for disaster; they feel de-charmed.

I delivered a commencement address on "Be Charming," in which I called to the attention of the audience the above superstitions. At the close of the address I joined the audience in some informal chatting. A railroad engineer approached me, with an air of having a mission, and said, "Well, that's something I've never had. I've never been superstitious." Thereupon he entered into a lengthy narration of his experiences as an engineer, citing one narrow escape after another, and then he concluded, "And, thank God, I've never once had an accident." With this he ceased his conversation, walked a few steps to a wooden door jamb and knocked upon it. As he came back, his facial expression made it quite clear that he felt safe from his brag. It is so easy to use charms and not recognize that we are doing it.[5]

The prediction of a fortune-teller may serve as a charm. The human being has always found the divining of the future most fascinating. His interest in it has been due primarily to his desire to feel that all things are going to work out for good in his life.

Mrs. I. S. had a series of misfortunes, and her imagination had been taken over by negative beliefs. Then she went to a diviner (fortune-teller, medium, or what-have-you) and was told, "Though things look dark now, it is always darkest just before the dawn; within the next five years you are going to come into a great fortune, and the dream of your life is going to come true."

Now, what happened to Mrs. I. S.'s imagination in this process? Obviously, since she believed what she had been told, it was shifted from a negative belief to a positive one. She left the fortune-teller with a feeling of "walking on air." She was charmed; she was visualizing herself in terms of success; for her, all things were working together for good. Little failures were of no consequence to her now. She was literally swallowed up in victory. As her imaginative experience became positive, gradually her faith-fear lifeline began to rise again. (Page 106.) The prophecies were a potent means of suggestion. It was true for her, so she achieved an invincible faith and worked it out.

Our belief in special endowments may be a "charm" for us. The early church practiced "anointing" as a means of healing, and some Christian groups continue the practice to this day. They use it because, not infrequently, people are healed. It must be noted that healing occurs, not because of the anointing, but rather because the patient is therewith stimulated to have an intense faith, and it is this faith that is packed with the power.

Some years ago I had a Protestant clergy friend who made use of the ash cross, placing it on the foreheads of his sick. He claimed many of his counsellees improved immediately and testified that their healing began with the sign of the cross on their foreheads. It is easy to see what happened. In the first place, my clerical friend believed that the ashes, through the benefit of his sacred office, had great (we might say, dynamic) healing power. He passed on his belief through the citing of cases where healing had taken place. In the person about to receive the ashes, a deep faith was aroused, and ofttimes the patient speedily turned for the better.

St. Peter gained such a reputation for healing that the sick lined the streets where he was to pass and were healed when the great man's shadow passed over them. They believed that his shadow would heal them, and then faithed themselves into being healed on the occasion of the shadow contact.

The blessed handkerchief sent to the sick with the claim that it will heal, and the candle burned in some sacred place, are ways of arousing faith-creating imaginative experiences in the people who believe in them, whether the devotee be Buddhist, Christian, or Hindu.

Oral Roberts, who by way of transcriptions conducted a healing radio program, used the idea of a radio wave as a charm. He asked people who were listening to his broadcast to touch their radios as a "point of contact" with him. He told them that when they did this, the power of healing would flow through them. We do not question but that it was faith with God that caused people to get well under Oral Roberts' ministry, but we must point out that the touching of the radio (as with anointing, laying on of hands, use of the ash cross, and so on) served only as a means to stimulate the faith-creating imaginative experience. It was the faith thus created that made them well.[6]

Everyone will have to evaluate the use of charms according to his own insights. It certainly is not the noblest technique of stimulating faith-creating imaginative experience.

Some years ago Harold L. Lloyd starred in a picture called "Grandma's Boy," which clearly illustrated the dangers of using a "charm" for creating faith. As I now recall, the grandson (played by Lloyd) was being reared by his grandmother. He was a timid, fear-ridden, ever-haunted Mr. Milquetoast-in-the-making youth. His grandfather, now dead, had been a soldier in the Civil War. Grandfather's portrait hung majestically over the fireplace mantel, and many were the stories that Grandma told the boy of his daring and fearless behavior. In fact, as Grandma described him, it seemed to the timid youth that his grandfather was everything that he, himself, wanted to be and was not.

Grandma sensed this, and it gave her an idea. She shared with her grandson the secret of his grandpa's success. It was this: he came through all of his dangers without a scratch because he had a charm that he carried wherever he went. Grandma's boy wanted it and Grandma produced it—a carved piece of bent wood. As Grandma gave it to her grandson, she assured him, with more stories from Grandpa's life, that when he carried that charm he would be simply invincible, even as was Grandpa.

What a changed and different person Grandma's boy became! He was Grandpa all over again. He was afraid of absolutely nothing and moved through life's experiences as easily as a snowplow empowered by a Sherman tank. And then, one day, Grandma's boy discovered that the charm was only an umbrella handle of much more recent vintage than Grandpa, and that he had been fooled. The charm was gone and so were his powers. His imagination dropped down to his former negative beliefs about himself, and the fear-ridden boy was back. *Those whose faith rests on the religious use of the charm find education a constant threat to their spiritual security.*

A much more sound and acceptable use of suggestion for the creating of imaginative experience is example.

Example

William James once said, "We draw new life from heroic example."

A chaplain in the Korean War gave new strength and courage to a panic-stricken soldier who was about to go into battle by promising to go with him.

Example leads to faith-creating imaginative experience on two counts. (a) It gives belief-creating evidence (page 67). Referring to the B.S.I. chart on page 96, the B.S.I. may read like this: "Because John Doe has done this, I believe that in this situation I, too, can succeed."

(b) By identification one imaginatively lives as, with, and in the example. One not only believes himself able to do as the example has done, but he feels himself doing it and thus creates faith.[7]

The author of *Cheaper by the Dozen,* Frank Gilbreth, through the contacts of his profession, met many people who were discouraged. Gilbreth formed the practice of keeping in his possession clippings concerning men and women who had overcome great handicaps—who had succeeded despite difficult situations. Whenever this efficiency engineer found a worker in industrial life facing a certain kind of problem, he would present him with the story of a man who had met a similar situation in a successful way. The effect, he said, was very good. The example gave the reader a new belief in his own possibilities and sent him away visualizing himself in terms of it.

Dr. Walter Athearn used to tell his classes at Boston University School of Theology of an experience in changing character through storytelling. A group of children were tested for honesty. They were given a chance to steal, not knowing that they were being watched. Practically all, if not all, did steal. During the following weeks they were not informed that they were being studied nor were they admonished not to steal, but during this period they were told stories in which honesty was practiced by the most admired and stealing was relegated to the behavior of the less desirable characters. At the end of the given period they were again tested. All came through with honest behavior save one girl, and she returned the money the next morning, greatly relieved at "coming clean." The examples in the stories gave the children a new honesty belief self-image and stimulated them to imagine themselves in terms of it. The time came when they *felt* honest and were honest.

A shrine is always couched in stories of healing, showing abandoned crutches, canes, braces, and so on, as evidence. The believer is led to imagine himself joining the procession of the cured. His imaginative experience is intense. In Jesus' day it was the practice of the sick to assemble at the pool of Bethzatha that they might be healed. It was believed that the first person to strike the water, after it was disturbed by the angel, would be healed. (John 5:2-9) It was always assumed that the one who was healed, or who claimed to be healed, was the one who first struck the disturbed water. (It is now believed that the pool had a natural siphon and that, being spring-fed, it would fill until it started the siphon and then would empty until the siphon sucked air, repeating the process over and over again.)

There was no healing power in the pool, of course, but there *was* power in the faith that it aroused in the folks seeking health. The example of others being healed stimulated many of the waiting sick to have an imaginative experience of being healed themselves, and out of this repeated and intensified experience came the faith that brought health to not a few.[8]

Charles Stevenson, writing of the rehabilitation of handicapped veterans, points out that faith is a matter of first importance in bringing the thrill back into the lives of the handicapped. They discovered that "example" was their best means of creating that faith.

A youngster, convalescing in bitter silence at Walter Reed Hospital, brightened up when a vivacious girl on the staff led him into conversation. He talked; she scribbled replies on a pad, for he was stone deaf.

"Won't you see me again?" he pleaded as she left. "It's awful not knowing what people around me are saying."

She smiled and wrote: "Oh, I don't think that it's so awful. I'm as deaf as you. Why not learn to read lips as I've been reading yours?"

Then there was the young Marine who crashed in a plane. They amputated both hands at the wrist. He grew more melancholy daily . . . until a visitor who made a show of flexing fingers, clenching his fists, lighting cigarettes and drinking coffee revealed his hands were plastic, realistic down to fingernails and skin-matching tint. They moved by cords attached to tendons in his arms. (3)

The impact of the examples served to create a positive B.S.I., and, through identification, the patient so lived with the hero as to find a new faith for living.

We all have heroes and heroines, and since from them we borrow our own belief self-image and, by much imaginative rehearsal, come to feel like them, who our heroes are and where we get them is of first importance, both to ourselves and to society. Dr. Karl Menninger points out that even what the therapist is may speak so loudly that the patient will not be able to hear what he says. He puts it this way:

We cannot ignore the fact that what the psychoanalyst believes, what he lives for, what he loves, what he considers to be the purpose of life and the joy of life, what he considers to be good and what he considers to be evil, become known to the patient and influence him enormously not as "suggestion" but as inspiration. A degree of identification with the analyst is inevitable, although not necessarily permanent. . . . No matter how skillful the analyst in certain technical maneuvers, his ultimate product, like Galatea, will reflect not only his handicraft but his character.

Menninger goes on to say:

A few years ago I participated in a seminar and panel discussion with some theologians, some professors of philosophy and of ethics, and some practicing psychoanalysts, who discussed the topic, "Do the Psychiatrist's Moral Convictions Play a Significant Part in His Psychiatric Therapy?" All of the speakers made definitely affirmative replies to the topical question. All of them felt that no psychiatrist would be able to avoid imparting his value system to his patients. (4)

This much is certain if the patient respects the psychiatrist. There was great insight in Jesus' invitation, "Follow me."

The advertiser knows all too well the power of personal example. When the envied and worshiped use a product, the public will want to use it, too. As a boy feels grown up when he puffs a cigarette, like an admired adult, so do ordinary people feel extraordinary when they use the products which the distinguished and extraordinary people use.[9]

Herein lie the assets and the liabilities of the story, the moving picture, and fiction. A child who is consistently told stories in which the hero or heroine acts on the level of brotherhood, love, prayer, and goodwill in solving his or her problems may there find the material that will lead to a gripping personal faith through faith-creating imaginative experience, stimulated by the fictional heroes and heroines. In fact, the hero of the drama or novel many times is a more potent stimulus to imaginative experience than the flesh-and-blood example because of the skill with which he is presented. All who are in search of faith do well to select their fiction and biographical company with great care.

It is the very nature of man to identify with his heroes. If our fictional heroes of television, cinema, and paperbacks are cheap and violent people, so will the people become who identify with them. It is alleged that there was a group who tested the sanity of a person by putting him in a tank, with no means of escape, and turned on a water faucet. They also gave him a bucket so that he could bail out the water as it ran in. If he labored to the point of exhaustion to bail out the water to keep from drowning instead of turning off the spigot, he was deemed insane. How long will it be before society has the sanity to turn off the spigot—by substituting fictional and dramatic examples worthy of the human race?[10]

Association

Association has great suggestive force in creating imaginative experience. I once knew a man who had what he thought at the time was a heart attack while making his rounds in the shop as a supervisor. One day he said to me, "Would you believe it? Every time I get near that place my heart starts to pound." We all have tainted places in our lives—places where we do not want to go because of the unwanted feeling that returns when we do.

A husband complained that his wife did not like to stay in one of the nicest hotels in a city which they frequently visited. When I inquired for the reason, he said with digust, "She says it's because that's the hotel where my first wife and I had our honeymoon. She says it spoils it for her." It no doubt spoiled it for the wife because she knew that it was spoiled for him. He could hardly be in that hotel without recalling some associations with another woman who was not his present wife. She instinctively knew that she would not be as much to him in that hotel as she would be in some other, whether he knew it or not.

Whereas "bad" associations shackle us to moods that we would escape, "good" associations stimulate us to get the substance of the things hoped for. This is the value of having a time and place for worship, both public and private. Where and when we have felt God, we will find it easier to feel him again.[11]

Affirmation

One of the most important ways of using suggestion (to obtain faith-creating imaginative experience) is affirmation. Affirmations are of two kinds: (a) personal (what we say to ourselves); and (b) directed (what is said to us by others). Both forms of affirmation are equally important and have a very definite place in achieving faith-creating imaginative experience.

Personal affirmation. When we think of the personal affirmation, the name of Coué comes first to mind. "Every day in every way I am getting better and better." This quote has come in for a lot of jeering, but we must not overlook its basic worth. Who is there who would dare to repeat, day after day, a negative affirmation such as, "I am losing my grip on life"? No surgeon would last long who affirmed, "I am getting shaky, unsteady, and losing my control." The weakness of Couéism was its oversimplification. The principle has its place in faith-centered living.

A few years ago Percy Westmore, New Zealand-born Hollywood cosmetic expert, said, "There is no such thing as an ugly woman. If every woman would completely forget her bad points and say to herself each day, 'I am the most beautiful woman in the world,' she would be on the way to becoming beautiful." This is, of course, an overstatement. But many a person who has felt accepted after a face-lifting operation has little realized how her changed attitude toward her face has contributed more to her acceptance than the operation itself. I had a sister-in-law (now dead) who, by all feminine standards, had a very unattractive face; but as you came to know her, you felt you were with a most charming person, for her face became lost in a magnificent spirit.

Dr. Walter Athearn, to whom we have made earlier reference, related the following experience from his teaching in an Iowa high school. He said that he sponsored in his school a "trial" of John Barleycorn. He chose an attorney for each side at random—two boys who were planning to enter the legal profession when they had finished law school. They were not chosen, he said, to take one side or the other for any reason except that there were two sides to be defended and two lawyers were needed. When these boys became men and attorneys-at-law, they locked horns on the liquor issue (over the passage of state laws to prohibit the sale of alcohol), and they were on exactly the same sides as they had been in high school at the trial of "John Barleycorn." Dr. Athearn observed that during his mock trial each of them had said, "I believe this" so often and so emphatically that, in the end, they had identified with the cause which they had been defending. They had established the pattern of their lives through the imaginative experience stimulated by personal affirmation (suggestion).

One should not pass over too lightly the fact that Marilyn Monroe, who took her life in August, 1962, did, in the course of her career, play the part of a suicide at Niagara Falls.

Jesus' use of personal affirmation. Jesus many times, I am sure, must have repeated such statements as these: "I and the Father are one"; "I am the light of the world"; "As God loves me, so love I you."

Paul's use of personal affirmation. Paul's affirmations would include such well-known texts as: "For me to live is Christ"; "I can do all things through Christ"; "Forgetting that which is behind, I press forward to my high calling in Christ Jesus."

The above personal affirmations were not only platforms on which Jesus and Paul stood but were also ladders on which they climbed. They stimulated faith-creating imaginative experience.[12] They were beliefs deeply felt.

The Psalmist's use of personal affirmation. If one wants to see the personal affirmation used at its best, he need but turn to the Twenty-third Psalm. The psalmist here asked for nothing but assumed everything to be true. He affirms:

The Lord is my shepherd; I shall not want.
He maketh me to lie down in green pastures:
He leadeth me beside the still waters.
He restoreth my soul: . . .

Take the affirmative language out of this Psalm and see what happens.

Lord, be my shepherd that I shall not want.
Make me to lie down in green pastures.
Lead me beside the still waters.
Restore my soul.
Lead me in the paths of righteousness for his name's sake
Even though I walk through the valley of the shadow
    of death,
Make me to fear no evil.
Give me a consciousness that you are with me.
Cause your rod and your staff to comfort me.
Prepare a table before me in the presence of mine enemies.
Anoint my head with oil.
Make my cup run over.
Assure me that goodness and mercy shall follow me all
    the days of my life, and that I shall dwell in the house
    of the Lord forever.

To break up this ancient affirmation in this way is to take the life out of it. It ceases to be faith-creating. It turns a masterpiece into something common.[13]

The Quaker use of personal affirmation. Thomas R. Kelly, a Quaker, in his *A Testament of Devotion* says:

There is no new technique for entrance upon this stage where the soul in its deeper levels is continuously at Home in Him. The processes of inward prayer do not grow more complex, but more simple. In the early weeks we begin with simple, whispered words. Formulate them spontaneously, "Thine only. Thine only." Or seize upon a fragment

of the Psalms: "so panteth my soul after Thee, O God."
Repeat them inwardly, over and over again. For the conscious
cooperation of the surface level is needed at first, before
prayer sinks into the second level as habitual divine orienta-
tion. (5)

To "repeat them inwardly" is personal affirmation at its best.
It brings the total mind into the faithing process as does the
Twenty-third Psalm.[14]

Personal affirmation in our hymns. The church has used the
personal-affirmation approach in its hymns more consistently
than it has any place else. How many times, as a boy, I used to
sing C. B. Martin's hymn, "God Will Take Care of You." I liked
it because, by the time I finished, I always felt God as caring
for me. The affirmation stimulated the faith-creating feeling of
being cared for. Whatever you think of these hymns, they have
their appeal because they are positive. They affirm the theme
as true. Who can sing Charles Wesley's "Christ the Lord Is Risen
Today" and not be lifted up with him? It is a hymn of affirmation, clinched by hallelujahs. "Made like Him, like Him we rise.
Hallelujah! Hallelujah!"

Or consider the words of Fanny Crosby's "Blessed Assur-
ance":

> Blessed assurance, Jesus is mine!
> Oh what a foretaste of glory divine!
> Heir of salvation, purchased of God!
> Born of His spirit, washed in His blood!

To sing Mary Lathbury's "Day Is Dying in the West" is to
feel quiet all over. You feel the sun setting.

> Day is dying in the west;
> Heaven is touching earth with rest;
> Wait and worship while the night
> Sets her evening lamps alight
> Through all the sky.

Personal affirmation and prayer. The most effective prayer takes the form of personal affirmation. Prayer, at its best, stimulates fellowship with God, shifting the imagination to the noblest beliefs about life through the language of the personal affirmation. To illustrate this, I would like to use a truly magnificent prayer written by Phillips Brooks. Read it carefully, meaningfully.

> Oh God, give me strength to live another day. Let me not turn coward before its difficulties or prove recreant to its duties. Let me not lose faith in my fellow men. Keep me sweet and sound of heart, in spite of ingratitude, treachery or meanness. Preserve me from minding little stings or giving them. Help me to keep my heart clean and to live so honestly and fearlessly that no outward failure can dishearten me or take away the joys of conscious integrity. Open wide the eyes of my soul that I may see the good in all things. Grant me this day some new vision of Thy truth; inspire me with the spirit of joy and gladness, and make me the cup of strength to suffering souls; in the name of the strong Deliverer, our Lord and Saviour, Jesus Christ. Amen.

When we frame this prayer in affirmative language, I think you will find that an effective prayer is made even more so.

> Oh God, our Father, as I turn to Thee in prayer, I sense strength to live another day and to live as nobly as I pray. Living with Thee this day, I will be brave before its difficulties and live worthily of its duties. To have faith in Thee is to have faith in my fellow men. I praise Thee for a sweet and sound heart; for the faith-sustaining ability to live above ingratitude, treachery or meanness. I thank Thee for a faith that makes me too big to be hurt by, or to give, little stings. Oh Thou Great Spirit, I feel Thee so close to my spirit that I know no outward failure can dishearten me or take away the joy of my conscious integrity. Thou hast opened the eyes of my soul. I see good in all things. God of Light, I turn this

day to some new vision of truth inspired by Thy love to a greater gladness. I sip with Thee the cup of strength to all suffering souls in the name of Him who had strength to overcome the world, even our Lord and Saviour, Jesus Christ. Amen.[15]

"Pray affirmatively," says Doctor Fosdick. "The trouble with much popular praying is that it is mainly begging. It conceives the Eternal as a universal organized charity and of ourselves as impecunious applicants, saying, 'Give me!'" He goes on to say that this is not only a pagan theory of God, but it does, in actual practice, damage men's souls.[16] (6)

Roy L. Smith, while editor of *The Christian Advocate* of the Methodist Church, suggested the use of personal affirmation in our devotional life. He says,

Call it what you will—autosuggestion, mental dope, controlled energy, prayer, mental therapeutics, aggressive faith or self-hypnosis—the beneficial results are in no wise altered by the name. . . .

Try asserting your faith the very last moment before sleep comes at nightfall. Saturate your mind with the great confessions of confidence; repeat the strongest passages of Scripture with which you are familiar; use the fleeting lines of great hymns that come across your mind. Do not plead with God but let your prayer be one of praise. Count up the blessings of the day and give thanks. Ignore your defeats and rejoice in your victories. Recount the joys of the day and postpone consideration of your anxieties until tomorrow. As you deliberately call up the blessings, mercies, joys, victories and happy memories of the day, you will find a sense of peace and satisfaction stealing in upon you, for that is the way faith works.[17] (7)

Those who have followed this advice in using the personal affirmation in devotion will be first to testify to its potency in stimulating faith-creating imaginative experience.

Dr. E. Stanley Jones' sixth step for receiving the Holy Spirit reads like this: "The acceptance of the gift of the Spirit . . . empty your hands and humbly take the Gift. Having given yourself, you have a right to take Himself. Then repeat to yourself, 'He comes—He comes. I let Him come. I welcome with open heart His coming. I am grateful for His coming. It is done. We belong to each other, forever.'"

Doctor Jones' seventh step is: "If you feel the inner urge, be free to tell others about His coming—share it."[18] (8)

Unconscious use of personal affirmation. Not unlike the young woman who touched the hem of Jesus' garment, we, too, affirm many things "within ourselves." The positions we hold—our social and family expectancies—all affect us, and we may not realize what is happening.

Some years ago Max Beerbohm published a story called "The Happy Hypocrite, a Fairy Tale for Tired Men," that illustrates in fiction what we have in mind.

Lord George Hell, who lived in London a long time ago, was thirty-five years old and not only was he wicked—he was proud of it and went to great lengths to be sure his escapades were well-publicized. His companion in his carousing was a dancer by the name of La Gambogi. One evening La Gambogi declared she was weary of the party they were attending and insisted on being taken to the theatre to see "The Fair Captive of Samarkand." A strange thing happened there. Lord George Hell looked upon an actress in the play, a young lady named Jenny Mere, and he fell in love. Being accustomed to getting anything he wanted, Lord George awaited Jenny Mere after the performance and, at once, offered her his wealth, rank, and of course, his love. Strangely enough Jenny refused them all. With gentle courtesy she explained, "I cannot be the wife of any man whose face is not saintly. Your face, my lord, mirrors what may be true love for me, but it is a tarnished mirror. You have great wealth, but my love must be given to that man whose face is as the saints. To him will I give my love."

That night Lord George Hell walked the dark streets of London, and his thoughts were as black as the night. Suddenly his whole life seemed to be a cage without bars. Dawn found him almost convinced that suicide was the only escape. His aimless wanderings had brought him to Bond Street, and he almost collided with fat Mr. Aeneas, the maskmaker, who was just unlocking his shop. In bitter jest Lord George asked, "Ah there, Sir maskmaker, can you make me the mask of a saint?" Now it just happened that Mr. Aeneas was a master of his trade, and he surprised Lord George by answering, "Certainly, will you have it with or without a halo?"

And, indeed, Mr. Aeneas did make such a mask, and it was a mask of a saint, a saint who loves dearly. The maskmaker asked Lord George how long he wished to wear the mask, and Lord George answered, "I must wear it until I die." With great care the maskmaker molded it to his client's face, and when he was, at last, finished and Lord George looked into the mirror, he beheld a new man, and suddenly his past life seemed as a dream. Thus abruptly, Lord George Hell disappeared from fashionable London society.

Wearing his mask, he presented himself again to Jenny and shortly heard her say, "Surely you are the good man for whom I have waited." They were married and, in his great happiness, Lord George felt a great need to atone, and quietly gave away most of his vast fortune. He was kind and gentle and good, as his Jenny believed he was.

Among his old cronies, only one recognized the quiet gentleman as the infamous Lord George Hell. That person was the dancer, La Gambogi. Consumed with jealousy, and that strange envy that compels evil to destroy good, she sought out their dwelling and told Jenny just what sort of a man she married. Jenny didn't believe a single word. Finally, infuriated by Jenny's absolute confidence in Lord George's goodness, La Gambogi sprang at him and tore the mask from his face. She uttered a cry of pure rage when she beheld his face, and then she rushed from the room.

Lord George, his mask hopelessly shattered, was alone

with his Jenny, and lo, his face was as the mask had been. Line for line, and feature for feature, it was the face of a saint—a saint who loves dearly. (9)

In this tale, George Hell demonstrated an eternal truth: *practice living as though* you are what you want to be (imaginatively as well as actually), AND YOU WILL BECOME SUCH. George Hell unconsciously used the personal affirmation as a means of stimulating faith-creating imaginative experience. Not only are we affected by what we say within ourselves but, also, by what others say to us.

Directed affirmation. A directed affirmation is that which we affirm to others or which they affirm to us. It is a way of describing a person to himself. We catch the impact of the directed affirmation most commonly in daily living—when we are either deprecated or complimented by someone.[19]

How readily we accept the judgments of others about ourselves as true (belief) and so clearly visualize ourselves in terms of them (imaginative experience) so as to destroy or create faith in ourselves!

The directed affirmation is especially useful in the counsellor-counsellee relationship.

Alson J. Smith explains how he used directed affirmation through the medium of the Scripture for instilling the will to live in a boy who was in a coma. When a young preacher serving in Montana, he was called to the sickbed of a boy seventeen years old. The patient had been ill with pneumonia for a long time, and the doctor felt he had brought the boy safely past the crisis, but the lad lay in bed, pale, listless, his vitality diminishing day by day even though his lungs cleared.

It was about two o'clock on a January morning when Doctor Smith received a call asking him to come out to the cabin where the boy lived. When he arrived, the doctor was having a cup of coffee in the kitchen. When Doctor Smith asked about Billy, he put down his cup and said, "I can't understand this case. I think he'll go any time now. Certainly before morning."

Then the physician went on to say that what Billy needed

was a kind of spiritual transfusion—something that would give him the will to live—or certainly he was going to die. "You've got to sell him on the idea that life is worth fighting for," he said. "And frankly, I don't think you can do it. Even if you could do it, I doubt if there's time now. He is in a coma, and I don't know whether you can get through to him or not." Smith said he did not know either.

Reverend Smith continued, "I hadn't the faintest idea what to say; where to begin. Billy's parents stood there beside the bed, waiting to see what I would do, and the clock ticked away the precious minutes of the boy's life. What did I do? The only thing I could do . . . I began to read from St. Paul's second letter to the Corinthians (the Short Bible translation):

> But I have this treasure in a mere earthen jar, to show that its amazing power belongs to God and not to me. I am hard pressed on every side, but never cut off; perplexed, but not driven to despair; routed, but not abandoned; struck down, but not destroyed; never free from the danger of being put to death like Jesus, so that in my body the life of Jesus also may be seen.
>
> So I never lose heart. Though my outer nature is wasting away, my inner is being renewed every day. For this slight, momentary trouble is piling up for me an eternal blessedness beyond all comparison, because I keep my eyes not on what is seen but what is unseen. For that which is seen is transitory, but what is unseen is eternal. . . .

"I read the Twenty-third Psalm, too, and prayed a little prayer for strength—not for deliverance, but just for strength. Finally Billy smiled and went from coma to sleep."

Doctor Smith stayed there the rest of the night, but finally he had to leave to make a hospital call fifty miles away. When he finished there, he called Billy's doctor, who said, "The transfusion was a success. Prognosis—good. I think the boy will pull through." (10) By directed affirmation Reverend Smith led Billy into the power-receiving experience of faith.

May I at this time (more in Chapter X) share one example from my personal practice of using the directed affirmation for the creating of faith? This is how the counsellee, Mrs. L. N., described it:

As I look back now, I am sure I did not realize how very, very depressed I had let myself become. I hated to be alone and yet was not decent company for anyone, and I guess I must have been a very frightened person.

After the first faithing session, I felt as though a load had been lifted from around my head, and my pain really seemed much less. I felt good and actually enjoyed just being alive.

Then when I discovered this other lump, it just seemed to be more than I could face; somehow it didn't seem worth the effort. After you came to the house and talked to me, I knew I would get up and go on to face whatever I had to, but perhaps not very heroically or cheerfully. I was doing things but, actually, evading thinking as much as possible.

But after the next session I had such a sense of well-being, I was interested in living and doing things—I could look ahead regardless of what might be there. I have been filled with such an inner glow. I haven't been able to describe it. At times I've wanted to; other times I've wanted to keep it as my own delicious secret; yet I'm sure this is something I should and will be able to share with others. It is an inner happiness, and I feel so close to God. I seem to be completely surrounded with his love.

When I remained in your study the other day, I achieved such a peace of mind. I'm confident I am going to be well. I can go about my daily living enjoying it—really. I'm all "bubbly" inside. Today (Thursday), when I rested, it seemed I could actually feel God's hand on me, and I fell into a deep, deep sleep. This is all a little more than I can comprehend. I feel very humble; am I worthy of this?

Friday is a wonderful day—is so good—filled to the brim, almost overflowing. I find myself offering up a silent prayer as I go about my work.

You will agree that this is religious experience at its best, but it was not something put over on her. She was aware of *how* and *what* we were trying to do at all times. It was for her a sense of God attained in a reasonable and predictable manner, through the use of the directed affirmation.

She had faithed in depth—had prayed in her total mind.

Not all response is as good as is the cases cited above. I am sure Doctor Smith would agree. The truth of the matter is that no two people, at either an opera or a football game, have the same feelings. Sometimes one feels that all effort is lost. I have come to see that the value is in almost direct ratio to the depth and the frequency of the faithing experience.

This principle comes clear as we observe fear as the opposite of faith. Fear will tear down and destroy in direct ratio to how intensely and frequently we feel ourselves getting the substance of the things not wanted. We may illustrate this with the figure below. The perpendicular lines are frequency; the cross lines are depth.

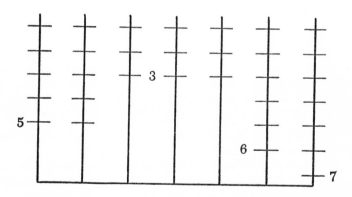

On seven successive directed-faithing sessions, the counsellee experienced a depth all the way from 1 to 7—and was helped in proportion. If the perpendicular lines represent days or weeks, the effect will be much greater than if they are months. To have a 1- to 3-depth experience often will do much more good than a 7-depth experience occasionally. The really life-changing faithing (religious experience) in most cases requires once or twice a week with not less than 4 to 5 in depth.[20]

NOTES

1. Do you argee that this is true because of the diversional nature of work?

2. I heard a young physician say that it seemed to him that the "colored aspirin" of the older doctors (with whom he was associated) did more good than his.

3. Discuss this matter of how a false belief may lead to faith.

4. Does this explain why so many differing psychological schools of thought are so successful?

5. What are some of the charms that you have in your life to help you have faith?

6. How do we degenerate such noble practices as tithing, Bible reading, and prayer into charms?

7. Illustrate these two facets of the suggestive power of example from your experience.

What does this say about the importance of heroes?

8. Show how example in this case served to create both the B.S.I. and faith.

9. Discuss example and how it is used by the advertiser.

10. How can this be done? Come up with some suggestions.

11. Can you think of some situations that have been spoiled for you because of bad associations?

12. How do you like to treat these statements—as recitation of fact or as great affirmation—or both? One is a theological assertion and the other is a means of creating faith.

13. How?

14. Discuss the place of the subconscious mind in this kind of personal affirmative praying and faithing.

15. Study the language of these two prayers. Try to restate the Brooks prayer yourself.

16. In what way does begging prayer damage men's souls?

17. How do Smith's thoughts fit into what we have been saying about "affirmation"?

18. Analyze these two steps for receiving the Holy Spirit in the light of our study of the affirmation. Note especially Step VII. What is the affirmative value of sharing?

19. Let us make sure we are clear on the difference between the personal and the directed affirmation and how they both lead to faith or fear.

20. In Part IV we will discuss the application of the directed affirmation for group and personal use. Make sure that all understand this figure.

Part IV

FAITH FOR TODAY

We have in a general way observed that, and how, beliefs are reason-made; that, and how, faith comes from experience (actual and imaginative). In these last chapters we wish to implement these findings for daily living.

We want to THINK, ACT, and FEEL as did Jesus in his relationship to God, self, others, and conditions about him—and we want to do it right where we are, in the "mud and scum of things." The procedure is but little different from that of an actor.

First, he must choose the person he is going to be in the drama (the part).

Second, he must practice his part, both imaginatively and actually, until he establishes character (feels it).

So in Chapter IX we shall set forth three steps by which one can decide where, specifically, he wants to be more Christian and who, in the light of his Christian beliefs, he believes he can be in that situation.

In the last chapter, we shall study a number of ways to practice being the person we have chosen to be and thus achieve faith—establishing Christian character.

CHAPTER IX

Establishing Our Hopes (Beliefs) for Daily Living

OUR QUEST: *A practical approach to finding the Christian belief self-image that belongs to a specific need.*

We come now to a very practical question: How do you, in a reasonable way, bring the religious experience into the practical affairs of life? How can you, as physician, clergyman, religious or public teacher, homemaker, attorney, counsellor, worshiper, parent, child, or businessman, make a faith-centered approach to daily living and assist those who seek your help in doing the same?

To make our quest more personal, let us suppose that someone said to you, "I want my religion to be more effective. I feel that I carry it more than it carries me." How would you help him?

Let us review some of the observations we have established that will be a part of our effort at achieving a faith (rather than a fear or neutral) approach to life.

1. The universal Christian dynamic is faith, the opposite of fear. (Chapter III)
2. Belief-creating is the intellectual side of religion. (Chapter V)
3. The belief self-image is the belief in which faith is rooted. (Chapter VII)
4. Faith comes from both actual and imaginative experience. (Chapter VIII)
    A. To experience a positive B.S.I. creates faith.
    B. To experience a negative B.S.I. creates fear.

5. Faith-creating imaginative experience may be achieved through the use of: (Chapter VIII)
   A. Diversion
   B. Reason
   C. Suggestion (charms—page 115; example—page 119; association—page 123; affirmation—page 124)
6. A Christian is one who relates in Jesus' way to God, self, others, and conditions about him. (Chapter II)

As we shake down these six observations into a formula for spiritual growth, we find that there are four important steps that will greatly assist us in our effort to gain Jesus' faith and thus relate to life in his way. As notes, by themselves, do not make music, neither are these four steps in themselves very exciting; but when prayerfully put together, the result will be most gratifying.

A member of my church was confronted with a very serious operation—so serious, in fact, that it called for the services of a surgeon and the equipment of a hospital some 150 miles away. He was to be there in one week. We talked it over, and he decided that he would like to work with me in making his case a faith experiment. To do so, I visited him each evening in his home to assist him in his faithing. A week or so later, his physician, who was with him during the operation, stopped me on the street and said, "I must share with you regarding Mr. K. He was the most faith-filled person I have ever seen. He said that you had helped him."

The four steps we are about to examine were used with Mr. K., but I am sure that he was not conscious of them as steps. There is nothing as effective as great music to make one forget the notes. Even so, as we make use of these four steps, as ways of moving to and through decisions to faith, I am well aware that there will be those who will dub them mechanical and artificial. And so they are, if faith is a gift; but if faith is an achievement (which I am sure it is), then it must be achieved, and where there is achievement, discipline and technique are of first importance.

The man whose pride is physical prowess must exercise discipline in order to be at his best. For the artist, talent is not enough; it requires long hours of practice and years of stubborn resistance to all temptations to accept less than the best for himself. One may have a high I.Q., but he will not be able to exploit his capacities without great discipline. He will have to live a disciplined life if he will be as much better than others in performance as he is in capacity. *So it is with faith.* We are all endowed with the capacity to faith, but for any of us to faith at our best will demand great discipline. No fair-minded person would expect to gain spiritual success with any less effort than it takes to attain other types of accomplishments.

As for technique, even lovemaking looks mechanical and artificial when broken down into its component parts; but those who counsel know, all too well, the many failures in lovemaking that would have been avoided had there been a deeper understanding and use of the fundamentals of the art.

No matter where we turn in religious practices, we come face to face with technique. For that matter, what are the practices of private worship, such as going apart, closing the eyes, or the reading of devotional literature (inculding the Bible), if they are not a technique of giving God a better chance in our lives? In mass evangelism, atmosphere was (I say *was* because I was brought up on it) all-important. The song leader had to do his part skillfully; the evangelist himself was technique in action. It is said of one of the great evangelists that, if he were going to have prayers from the audience, he always asked at least six people beforehand to pray first. This technique had a way of getting things off to a good start. It guaranteed enthusiasm.

Jesus sent his disciples out two by two, a method that was certain to assist them in having greater confidence than if they traveled alone. He urged upon these first callers the need to keep going. He even gave them a ritual by which they could extricate themselves from the influence of public indifference to their message. "Shake off the dust from your feet," he said, "and go to the next village." (Matt. 10:14 R.S.V.)

One would be well within the facts to say that all men have a technique of creating the faith experience (getting a new grip on life when they have lost it). These four steps, as so many have told me after studying and practicing them, help one to understand what he is doing and how. I was teaching a class in which a minister, of a somewhat different theological stance than mine, was a member. After I had sketched the four steps, he commented that they could be successfully used by those of any theological outlook. My reply was that if his observation was not correct, then the approach was wrong. As Christians we should never rest until we have found the best and most scientific way of creating the faith experience. May we say again that some of the methods employed by the church to create and harness faith are not unlike the house-burning method of roasting a pig in Charles Lamb's story. Though in a way effective, they are roundabout—not to mention expensive—means of getting results. I pray that you will find these four steps both direct and effective.[1]

THE FOUR STEPS

We shall consider "the four steps" in more detail later, but let me introduce each of them with a brief statement.

Step I: Where

This brings us face to face with our definition of a Christian by asking, "Where do I want to relate in Jesus' way better than what I am now doing?" (to God, self, others, and conditions)

Step II: What

What are my present negative feelings in this area of failure (Step I), and why do I feel as I do?

Step III: Who

Who do I want to be, where I am now failing, and why do I think I can be this kind of a person?

Step IV: How

Creating the faith self-image by bringing the decisions of Steps I and III into both actual and imaginative practice.

THE FOUR STEPS DIAGRAMMED

This effort to show the four steps in diagrammatical form should prove helpful. As you study it, it will be apparent that the first three steps are decision-making (WHERE, WHAT, WHO), whereas the last is faith-creating through the prayerful practice of the decision. (From experience comes faith.) The fourth and last step (HOW) is so important that we have set aside a chapter for its study. (See charts on pages 144-147.)

The Importance of Decision

The religious experience is, indeed, a sense of being "saved." It is a feeling of being secure within oneself, in love with one's neighbor, master over or in conditions, and at one with God. And this (as our mass evangelists so consistently remind us) begins with a decision. Not even God can make us into the person that we do not choose to be.

One of the assumptions of Sigmund Freud in psychoanalysis has been that man tends to rationalize things; that is, he tends to do things and then give reasons for doing them, like the fellow who shot a bullet in the fence and then drew the bull's-eye around it. This much is true: If one does not reason out what he wants to be, he will use reason to rationalize what he is. For some, the account of the rich young man turning away from Jesus (Mark 10:17-22) dramatized Jesus' failure as a counsellor; for others it said, "We are all free to choose. We may even turn our backs on Jesus."

Depth psychology taught us to recognize the present in terms of the past. It is equally important, if not more so, to recognize that future is determined by our present decisions. We are, indeed, stabbed by Viktor Frankl's statement that man, rather

Decision One

STEP I   WHERE

Where, specifically, do you choose to improve your relating to God, Self, Others, or Conditions?

BELIEFS

Religious	General
1—God	Ability—13
2—Jesus	Education—14
3—Bible	Position—15
4—Holy Spirit	Appearance—16
5—Prayer	Handicap—17
6—Faith	Money—18
7—Immortality	Clothes—19
8—Man	Experience—20
9—Church	failure—a
10—Evil	success—b
11—Intuitive awareness	Health—21
12—Charms	Personality—22
	Family—23
	Example—24

Because of my belief about "X" and "O"

I believe that in my relationship

to (WHERE—Step I)

I can be (WHO—Step III-A)

YOUR BELIEF SELF-IMAGE

144

STEP II	Decision Two	WHAT		STEP III	Decision Three	WHO

What is your present Feeling Self-Image in your selected improvement area?

Who do you want to be in your chosen improvement area? (Your new B.S.I.)

A	B	A	B
DESCRIPTIVE WORDS— NEGATIVE	Why do you think you feel as you do in this area?	DESCRIPTIVE WORDS— POSITIVE	Reasons for believing it is possible for you to relate this way

CREATING YOUR FAITH SELF-IMAGE

Changing knowledge into feeling—beliefs into faith. Proverbs 23:7

DECISION IN REVIEW

1. Where did you decide to be more Christian? (Step I—write in B below.)
2. What words best describe the kind of person you chose to be in your improvement area? (Step III-A—write in A below.)
3. Which beliefs (1-24) undergird your new Belief Self-Image?
4. How do you expect to practice your new B.S.I. (actually and imaginatively)?

BRINGING YOUR DECISIONS INTO PRACTICE

1. PREPARATION

A. Physically

Attain a comfortable position, either sitting or reclining. Relaxation is very desirable. Portions of the services on pages 188, 189 should be helpful.

B. Mentally—be still and receive.

Think of yourself as being as still and as quiet as light. Remember that God has something great for you, and that all you have to do is to accept it. Affirm God's power (Holy Spirit, Grace, Presence) as permeating your whole being. Think on these things: Luke 7:7, 24:49; Phil. 2:3; John 1:2; Acts 2:15; Eph. 2:7, 8.

2. GOD-CENTERED IMAGINATIVE PRACTICE (including what you expect to do actually)

A. Accept God's power as filling your total mind (conscious and subconscious).

B. Affirm the creative power of God in your total mind as making you:

THIS KIND OF PERSON ➤

WHEN IN THIS SITUATION ➤

A

B

Affirm each descriptive word (A) one at a time, several times in the situation (B). Seek to identify with the person that you have chosen to be.

The closing prayer may be thus: "God, our Father, I accept your spirit in my total mind as making me the person I have chosen to be. As I have practiced and lived in my mind, so I am going to live with my hands, feet, and lips. I know that as you were in Jesus, so you are in me. In His spirit I pray. Amen."

3. GOD-CENTERED ACTUAL PRACTICE

Making and taking every opportunity to be a doer of the Word. As much as possible, to do actually what you have done imaginatively and to affirm God in your life as you do it.

than being a sublimated animal, "can demonstrate that he conceals within himself a repressed angel." (1) As a dynamic exception to environmental determinism, man can always remain a human being. He can choose to be a saint. He does not, under any circumstances, have to be a swine.

In the year 1830, or thereabouts, a government employee by the name of George Wilson killed a man who caught him robbing the mails. At his trial, he was sentenced to be hanged. President Andrew Jackson sent him a pardon, but Wilson refused it. The case was then referred to the Supreme Court and Chief Justice Marshall wrote the opinion. "A pardon is a slip of paper, the value of which is determined by the acceptance of the person to be pardoned. If it is refused, it is no pardon. George Wilson must be hanged." (2)

It is a promise of spiritual health when we see that all of the power, grace, and love of God demonstrated in Jesus' life is available for us, even as it was available to him; but we must chose to receive and use it. Christian relatedness, even with God, begins with decision.[2]

In the light of this, we now turn to examine the first three steps in some detail.

Step I—WHERE (page 144). Making up our mind *where* we want to be more mature.

A seven-year-old boy hurt his leg, and his mother took him to a masseur. She let him go into the office alone while she remained in the waiting room. While she was still listening for his screams, out he came and announced that he was ready to go home. As they walked down the street, the mother congratulated him on his pluck. "Why," she said, "you never even groaned!"

"Huh," said the lad, "you don't think that I gave him my bad leg, do you?"

We are all apt to do this. It is not easy for any of us to face our problem. Even to ourselves we are deceptive. As we said before, there is great truth in the Freudian assumptions that irrational emotions are at the root of most of man's behavior, and one of his primary tendencies is to rationalize his behavior. If one will mature in his relation to any phase of life, he must begin with the clear recognition of *where* he wants to improve.

When Jesus met the paralytic of thirty-eight years at the pool of Bethzatha, he asked, "Do you want to be healed?" (John 5:2-9, R.S.V.) Our Lord knew that being sick, and even being at the place of healing, was not proof positive that the paralytic wanted to be healed. If we will relate to life in Jesus' way, we must decide that—and where—we want to get well.

J. L. had spent much time and considerable money seeking help for what seemed like physical trouble. As a part of her search for health, she came to me, as she had gone to many others, looking for a magician. After some sessions, I asked her if she was sure that she really wanted to get well. She resented my question and decided, after some further discussion, not to come back. Before she left, however, I tried to impress upon her that I was on her side, and that if she ever thought I could help her, she should look me up.

Time passed, and then a letter came from her requesting an appointment, with the explanation that she had received divine healing. When she came to my study, it seemed clear that the divine healing was emotional, saving her face, and that now she was free to get well. I have worked with few people who responded so readily as did she to her therapy. Wanting to get well made the difference between sickness and health in her case. We must be willing to give our bad leg to the doctor!

Step II—WHAT (page 145). Present feeling self-image. Making up our mind just what our feelings are in this area of our immaturity and why.

In this second decision, one must ask himself quite frankly, "What are my feelings now in this area where I have chosen to mature my relationship, and why do I feel as I do?"

There are two widely differing schools of thought concerning the importance of Step II. The Freudian school assumes that all attitudes are rooted in past experiences, and it is in these past experiences that we must search for the real reasons for our present feelings. As they see it, to bypass this second step, in any kind of therapy, would be as ridiculous as it would be for a physician to try to heal a wound without extracting the splinter. Not everyone, but many, will need outside help in order to find and remove the cause of the infection. It may be a friend, physician, pastor, or psychiatrist. It will all depend on how deep the "splinter" has gone.

If we share this view, it will help to clarify the second step if we jot down some words that describe our true feelings. If it is a person toward whom we seek better relations, we may find that such words as "hate," "fear," "shame," "jealousy," and "guilt" describe our feelings about them; then we proceed, by whatever help available, to face honestly the reasons why we feel as we do.

To be honest here will test our integrity. It is so delightful to think of others (not ourselves) as being responsible for what we are. A wholesome way to approach this is to ask frankly, "Where have I permitted myself to become victim rather than being master in my relationship to my environment of self, others, or conditions?" Others may have had much to do with what we are, but we must go slow in blaming them. To approach responsibility (blame) with honesty will do much to clarify the "what and why" of our negative feelings.

Step III—WHO (page 145). Creating a new belief self-image. We are confronted with the final and big decision: Who do I want to be in this area where I have broken down, and why do I think I can be this kind of person?

In trying to bring this step into focus, we could do no better than to follow closely, and quote rather extensively, psychiatrist Dr. William Glasser, who practices what he chooses to call "Reality Therapy." He says that people belong to one of two groups: the responsible or the irresponsible. The responsible people are those who have the ability to fulfill their needs—"and to do so *in a way that does not deprive others of the ability to fulfill their needs.*" Says Doctor Glasser,

Indeed, if the ability to fulfill our needs were as much a part of man as are the needs themselves, there would be no psychiatric problems. A Chinese infant girl has the same needs as a Swedish king. . . . Psychiatry must be concerned with two basic psychological needs: *the need to love and be loved and the need to feel that we are worthwhile to ourselves and to others.* . . . We know, therefore, that *at the time any person comes for psychiatric help he is lacking the most critical factor for fulfilling his needs, a person whom he genuinely cares about and who he feels genuinely cares about him.* . . .

Fulfilling his needs, however, is a part of his present life; it has nothing to do with his past no matter how miserable his previous life has been.[3] It is not only possible, it is desirable to ignore his past work, work in the present, because, contrary to almost universal belief, nothing which happened in his past, no matter how it may have affected him then or now, will make any difference once he learns to fulfill his needs at the present time.

Having established that we are concerned with involvement and what the patient is doing now in contrast to the usual emphasis on his past life, we must also state that we do not concern ourselves with unconscious mental processes. We do not deny that they exist as demonstrated vividly by our dreams, but they are unnecessary to the essential process of helping a patient fulfill his needs, a process which we have found must be completely conscious to be effective. (3)

This view is supported by the results they have obtained when using it in the Ventura School for older adolescent girls in the Santa Clara Valley of California. They claim success with 80 percent of their girls. As an example, Linda stayed about six months in the school, and before she left she was asked to write a summary of her experiences in institutions and with psychiatric treatment in general. Here is what she wrote.

During the past three years I have been under a variety of psychotherapists and, in this time, I have experienced a number of different attitudes toward myself and towards those who surround me. My first psychiatrist was a rather large shoulder-to-cry-on type. . . . She convinced me that I was emotionally disturbed and, therefore, was not to be held responsible for my actions. . . . Since it was on my record that I was an emotionally disturbed child, there were various exceptions made for me on this premise. I was not to be upset as I became violent and even masochistic at times. . . . It was at this point in my life that I learned the advantages of being emotionally disturbed and I played them to the fullest advantage. I was upset a lot and managed to time these little episodes to get in or out of most of the difficulties that were encountered.

I then entered a school full of girls like myself who had been either in minor or major difficulties. They ranged from assault and prostitution cases to run-away and sex delinquency. But we were all upset quite often and found this to be a clear reason for anything we did. After all, we were the emotionally disturbed and high strung delinquents and this made any and all things we did excusable. We had both private and group therapy. These were sessions in which each girl relived all the frustrations and disturbances. We were allowed the excessive use of profanity, even when directed towards members of the Staff. We were not required to give any of the respect their positions demanded. It was through these various therapy sessions that the girls managed to manipulate the staff into their way of thinking and would mold the rules to comply with what they wanted.

Shortly before my release from that institution I struck a staff member and instigated a riot which got me sent to California Youth Authority and found that these people had an extremely different attitude toward the girls. So you were emotionally disturbed, so big deal! There wasn't anything that anyone but you could do about it so why worry. I was there under the therapy of Dr. Glasser and Mr. Toobert. I found that Dr. Glasser was less interested in what you had done in your past than he was in your immediate and far future. He was a very personable man and he gave you the feeling that he was interested in you, but not what you had done, and never implied that there was any reason to ask "why" as there was no fact necessary but that you did it and that was the reason for your present incarceration. However, there was not any excuse for what you had done and you were to hold no one else responsible for your actions. This is good for it makes you accept the responsibility rather than give the fault to everyone who helped compose your environment. Now I am leaving Ventura Y. A. in a matter of days. I have learned that I cannot alter the past but can control my future and the responsibility lies solely with me as to my future. (4)

Linda had learned what we all must learn if we will make a faith approach to life. We must decide who we want to be. It will do much to clarify this step if the seeker will write down some three to six carefully examined words in the space provided (III-A) on the chart on page 145 which describe the person he really wants to be. He will do well to write in pencil so that he can replace words which more reflection have proven to be inaccurate, not to mention dishonest.

The second part of Step III is of special significance to Christians asking: "Why do I think I can be this kind of person in this area (Step I) of my immaturity?" Here we create the belief self-image, out of our personal religious beliefs as well as our general beliefs. Religious beliefs should make a real difference. Certainly what one believes about God, Jesus, the Holy Spirit, prayer, and the Bible will greatly determine what he can dare to believe about himself.

Note again the chart on page 154.

Check the beliefs (X and O) on both sides that make up your belief self-image, making sure that they are honest by discussing them with a trusted person. It would seem that those who are of the church would think first of their pastor at this time.[4]

```
┌─────────────────────────────────────────────────────┐
│                        BELIEFS                        │
│                                                       │
│      Religious                          General       │
│     1—God           ☐        ☐          Ability—13    │
│     2—Jesus         ☐        ☐        Education—14     │
│     3—Bible         ☐        ☐         Position—15     │
│     4—Holy Spirit   ☐        ☐       Appearance—16     │
│     5—Prayer        ☐        ☐        Handicap—17      │
│     6—Faith         ☐        ☐          Money—18       │
│     7—Immortality   ☐        ☐         Clothes—19      │
│     8—Man           ☐        ☐      Experience—20      │
│     9—Church        ☐        ☐          failure—a      │
│    10—Evil          ☐        ☐         success—b       │
│    11—Intuitive              ☐          Health—21      │
│       awareness     ☐        ☐      Personality—22     │
│    12—Charms        ☐        ☐          Family—23      │
│                              ☐         Example—24      │
│                          ▲                            │
│  ─────────────────────────────────────────────────   │
│  Because of my belief about "X" and "O"               │
│  ─────────────────────────────────────────────────   │
│  I believe that in my relationship                    │
│  ─────────────────────────────────────────────────   │
│  to (WHERE—Step I)                                    │
│  ─────────────────────────────────────────────────   │
│  I can be (WHO—Step III-A)                            │
│  ─────────────────────────────────────────────────   │
│             YOUR BELIEF SELF-IMAGE                    │
└─────────────────────────────────────────────────────┘
```

Three Steps Illustrated: The case of L. R. and his son, T. R., will serve to summarize the first three steps and lead us to the use of the fourth step (HOW), to be studied in the next chapter.

Mr. L. R. approaches the counsellor because he senses a breakdown of relations between himself and his fifteen-year-old son, T. R. Mr. L. R. has been a marked success in his profession; he worked hard to get there and is not a little proud of both the ladder and the rung on which he stands. None of this seems important to T. R. His grades are passing, but barely so. He skips school on occasion; has been suspected of taking money from the family till; lies to his parents about his whereabouts;

and, when cornered, shrugs it off. He is the son they got, not the one they wanted or expected. Mr. L. R. is convinced that he is becoming a problem parent, even as T. R. is a problem youth.

Needless to say, I had a number of counselling sessions with both L. R. and T. R. Mr. L. R. was given the four-step worksheet, and we worked it out together.

Under *Step I—Where?* (page 158), he concluded that it was at the point of his son's deficiencies, such as his lack of ambition and inability to learn. He felt that, somehow, he needed to adjust himself to this reality, and so we wrote under Step I: "Creative relationship with my fifteen-year-old son at the point of his deficiencies." L. R. was convinced that unless he could do this, his son would not only fall below his hopes for him, but below his abilities as well.

We turned next to L. R.'s present feeling self-image (Step II, page 159) as he considered T. R.'s failures. We settled for the following descriptive words, each of us writing them on our worksheet: *humiliated, frustrated, resenting, hating.* We considered why he felt this way. As we talked this over, he concluded that it was due partly to his pride in his own success. He was frank to say that he had always looked down on people who did not get ahead, and that T. R. seemed to drop below his ability in almost everything he did.

We turned now to the third step and considered the kind of parent L. R. would like to be, no matter how his son behaved. As he put it, "The worse things are, the more a parent is needed at his best." After much discussion, he suggested the following descriptive words (Step III-A, page 159): *understanding, loving, objective, encouraging, parental.* (This last word meant something special to him.)

I asked L. R. if he had any reason for thinking he could be that kind of father. He felt that he should make this a special project; he would make it his business to do it—as he had learned to play golf; he could do anything that he made up his mind to do. I ventured the suggestion that he had tried the "make yourself do it" approach before, and that it had not worked. L. R.

slumped down in his chair as he said, "You're quite right. Those words are just fanciful dreams, aren't they?"

It was here that I suggested that we think about God and faith and Jesus' approach to life's situations. We shared our views of God, agreeing that he does—or should—make a difference in our lives; that working with him in Jesus' way will enable us to do what we could not do alone. L. R. said he was sure that if he were to be "parental," he would need some help from the Great Parent.

Now we considered the creating of a new faith (feeling) self-image (Step IV); whereas he had made a fear approach to his son in the past, he now wanted to make a faith approach. We each filled in the spaces "A" and "B" at the bottom of Step IV-A, page 161 (how). In "A" we wrote: *understanding, loving, objective, encouraging, parental.* In "B" we wrote: *when T. R. fails.*

We now discussed how faith is created by both actual and imaginative experience, using the idea of the chart on page 109, illustrating the three lines with my three fingers. We considered how Mr. L. R. would have to enter into this faith-creating imaginative and actual experience. His worksheets are shown on pp. 158-161.

NOTES

1. Discuss some of the techniques used by members of the group to get up when they are down—to get back "on the beam," as it were.

2. Review the three decision steps and ponder their significance (pages 144-45).

3. Note the different emphasis here from that of Freudism.

4. If your group has come to the place of trust and frank speaking, you may work in small groupings or as a whole group.

STEP I   Decision One   WHERE

Where, specifically, do you choose to improve your relating to God, Self, Others, or Conditions?

Creative relationship with my 15-year-old son — at the point of his deficiencies.

BELIEFS

Religious	General
1–God ☒	Ability–13 ◨
2–Jesus ☐	Education–14 ☐
3–Bible ☐	Position–15 ☐
4–Holy Spirit ☐	Appearance–16 ☐
5–Prayer ☒	Handicap–17 ☐
6–Faith ☐	Money–18 ☐
7–Immortality ☐	Clothes–19 ☐
8–Man ☐	Experience–20 ☐
9–Church ☐	failure–a ☐
10–Evil ☐	success–b ☐
11–Intuitive awareness ☐	Health–21 ◨
12–Charms ☐	Personality–22 ☐
	Family–23 ☐
	Example–24 ◨

Because of my belief about "X" and "O"

I believe that in my relationship

to (WHERE–Step I) *My son*

I can be (WHO–Step III-A)

YOUR BELIEF SELF-IMAGE

Decision Two WHAT		Decision Three WHO	
STEP II What is your present Feeling Self-Image in your selected improvement area?		STEP III Who do you want to be in your chosen improvement area? (Your new B.S.I.)	
A DESCRIPTIVE WORDS— NEGATIVE	B Why do you think you feel as you do in this area?	A DESCRIPTIVE WORDS— POSITIVE	B Reasons for believing it is possible for you to relate this way
Humiliated Frustrated Resentful Hating	Personal pride of success Personal ambition	Understanding Loving Objective Encouraging Parental	Success with others not family Personal pluck God's spirit
Attitude toward "failures"		Other parents do this	

CREATING YOUR FAITH SELF-IMAGE

Changing knowledge into feeling—beliefs into faith. Proverbs 23:7

DECISION IN REVIEW

1. Where did you decide to be more Christian? (Step I—write in B below.)
2. What words best describe the kind of person you chose to be in your improvement area? (Step III-A—write in A below.)
3. Which beliefs (1-24) undergird your new Belief Self-Image?
4. How do you expect to practice your new B.S.I. (actually and imaginatively)?

BRINGING YOUR DECISIONS INTO PRACTICE

1. PREPARATION

A. Physically
   Attain a comfortable position, either sitting or reclining. Relaxation is very desirable. Portions of the services on pages 188, 189 should be helpful.

B. Mentally—be still and receive.
   Think of yourself as being as still and as quiet as light. Remember that God has something great for you, and that all you have to do is to accept it. Affirm God's power (Holy Spirit, Grace, Presence) as permeating your whole being. Think on these things: Luke 7:7, 24:49; Phil. 2:3; John 1:2; Acts 2:15; Eph. 2:7, 8.

2. GOD-CENTERED IMAGINATIVE PRACTICE (including what you expect to do actually)

A. Accept God's power as filling your total mind (conscious and subconscious).

B. Affirm the creative power of God in your total mind as making you:

THIS KIND OF PERSON ➡

WHEN IN THIS SITUATION ➡

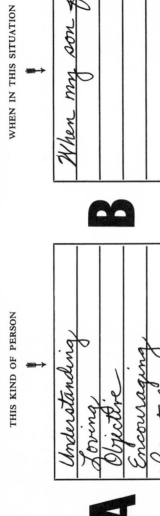

A	B
Understanding	When my son fails
Loving	
Objective	
Encouraging	
Parental	

Affirm each descriptive word (A) one at a time, several times in the situation (B). Seek to identify with the person that you have chosen to be.

The closing prayer may be thus: "God, our Father, I accept your spirit in my total mind as making me the person I have chosen to be. As I have practiced and lived in my mind, so I am going to live with my hands, feet, and lips. I know that as you were in Jesus, so you are in me. In His spirit I pray. Amen."

3. GOD-CENTERED ACTUAL PRACTICE

Making and taking every opportunity to be a doer of the Word. As much as possible, to do actually what you have done imaginatively and to affirm God in your life as you do it.

CHAPTER X

Getting the Substance
of Our Hopes

OUR QUEST: *A practical approach to changing "head know-ing" into "heart knowing" for daily living (decisions into feelings) through practice.*

T. H. Huxley, an agnostic in his approach to religion, wrote to Charles Kingsley, "The longer I live the more obvious it is to me that the most sacred act of a man's life is to *say* and *feel*, 'I believe such and such to be true.'"

How true this is! We must not only have beliefs (must make up our minds), but our beliefs must have us (making up our hearts). The spiritually immature may have beliefs as good as or better than a lot of other people's, but they never experience them. One cannot understand either a country or a belief until he has lived in it. In this chapter we want to consider the "how" of turning decisions into feelings; belief self-images into faith self-images. We are wisely admonished not to be just hearers, but doers, of the word, for only as we do the word can we feel the word. It is from the experience of doing (actual and imaginative) that we get our faith. It is a very simple formula. Think like a Christian and act like a Christian until you feel like one.

Actual Doing

Actually doing something is vital to creating faith. When the seeker after faith has made the decisions of the first three steps, he must now take every opportunity to practice his beliefs in living situations. As an example, if he has decided to be more Christian in his relation to other races (Step I), then he must consciously live that way in as many actual racial situations as possible and as often as possible. He who will be proficient in anything must exploit every opportunity to be an actual doer of it, for there is no experience as potent as this in creating faith.

The emphasis on imaginative experience, which is to follow, should not be interpreted as a deprecation, in any way, of the importance of the actual "doing the word," but rather as a realistic insight into the fact that most of us will have little success in making "up our hearts" unless we supplement our actual with imaginative practice of our beliefs. In Chapter VII we considered the means of creating imaginative experience. In review, they are:

1. Diversion
2. Reason
3. Suggestion
   a. Charms
   b. Example
   c. Association
   d. Affirmation (personal and directed)

As we turn to the practical application of these in achieving faith-creating imaginative experience, we shall find ourselves using them all in various degrees of intensity. We will not be surprised to discover that reason and suggestion are the most commonly used, and that under the latter, it will be example and affirmation which will meet our needs the most often.

Directed Affirmation—as an effective means of achieving faith-creating imaginative experience.

As we use the directed affirmation, we must keep in mind that the ultimate goal of faithing in depth through directed affirmation is that the participant will learn how to reach the same depth (or nearly so) by personal affirmation.

As the counsellor and counsellee proceed in the use of the directed affirmation (page 132), they will want to make sure that they are in agreement regarding the decisions made in Steps I-III. They may then proceed with the Step IV format.

It should be said, further that the best results will be obtained when the procedural format is given directional

STEP IV

CREATING YOUR FAITH SELF-IMAGE

Changing knowledge into feeling—beliefs into faith. Proverbs 23:7

DECISION IN REVIEW

1. Where did you decide to be more Christian? (Step I—write in B below.)

2. What words best describe the kind of person you chose to be in your improvement area? (Step III-A—write in A below.)

3. Which beliefs (1-24) undergird your new Belief Self-Image?

4. How do you expect to practice your new B.S.I. (actually and imaginatively)?

BRINGING YOUR DECISIONS INTO PRACTICE

1. PREPARATION

A. Physically

Attain a comfortable position, either sitting or reclining. Relaxation is very desirable. Portions of the services on pages 188, 189 should be helpful.

B. Mentally—be still and receive.

Think of yourself as being as still and as quiet as light. Remember that God has something great for you, and that all you have to do is to accept it. Affirm God's power (Holy Spirit, Grace, Presence) as permeating your whole being. Think on these things: Luke 7:7, 24: 49; Phil. 2:3; John 1:2; Acts 2:15; Eph. 2:7, 8.

2. GOD-CENTERED IMAGINATIVE PRACTICE (including what you expect to do actually)

A. Accept God's power as filling your total mind (conscious and subconscious).

B. Affirm the creative power of God in your total mind as making you:

THIS KIND OF PERSON   WHEN IN THIS SITUATION

A	B

Affirm each descriptive word (A) one at a time, several times in the situation (B). Seek to identify with the person that you have chosen to be.

The closing prayer may be thus: "God, our Father, I accept your spirit in my total mind as making me the person I have chosen to be. As I have practiced and lived in my mind, so I am going to live with my hands, feet, and lips. I know that as you were in Jesus, so you are in me. In His spirit I pray. Amen."

3. GOD-CENTERED ACTUAL PRACTICE

Making and taking every opportunity to be a doer of the Word. As much as possible, to do actually what you have done imaginatively and to affirm God in your life as you do it.

165

importance only and the counsellor proceeds with great freedom and confidence. For example (when the counsellee is in a comfortable position sitting or reclining), the counsellor may begin thus: "M. C., it is clear to both of our minds the kind of person you want to be and where. Will you now please close your eyes and tell your body to become still—completely still? Now raise your right leg two inches and hold it there until told to drop it, or you feel you have to." (This is also done, in turn, with the left leg and both arms. There should be no hurrying at this point; keep talking in terms of the heaviness of the limbs.) "Your body is overflowing with quietness; absorbed in stillness; completely surrendered. It is heavy; it is as though it were not yours; it is as though it were not a part of you. You will now, forgetting your body (take time to attain relaxation), move from the conscious to the subconscious mind—

from the outer to the inner mind;
from having to being;
from things to thoughts;
from thinking to feeling;
from the senses to the soul;
from strife to surrender;
from time to eternity.

"You are one with God. You feel and accept the power of God as flooding your total mind. Guided and empowered by the spirit of God, in your total mind, you have become a prayer. You are the person that you want to be (the descriptive words of IV-A should be used here) and where (note the specific place—IV-B). As you lie here in physical abandonment, you feel the tide of power coming into your whole being. As you yield (IV-B—state the situation of concern), you feel the power of God in your inner mind, literally *making* you (just one of the descriptive words of IV-A); you are leavened from within. You feel invincible—you are master. (Follow the same format for the other descriptive words—use them separately and together. Help the counsellee to experience living in IV-B on the level of these descriptive words (IV-A) as often and with as much depth as possible.) Think of this God power and love in your total mind . . . crowding all evil (be specific) out of your life. You are overcoming evil with good. Now you are free to be your greatest self . . . even as had Jesus so have you. You are alive as he was alive . . . you are truly free." (The motif here is for the counsellor and counsellee to have discovered what kind of person the counsellee wants to be and where, and then for the counsellor to help the counsellee to feel himself, through the power of God in the total mind, as being made into that person).

"This is a sacred experience, a holy place to which you can come back as often as you choose and under your own direction. All you have to do is become quiet of body and receptive of mind, and God will flood your whole being.

"M. C., you are now to move from the inner to the outer mind; but as you do, you know that what you have experienced will remain permanently to guide and empower you, that you will always be guided and empowered from within. You are a new person—forever new. You can vividly feel yourself living empowered. Sensations are coming back into your legs and arms —you are moving from—

thoughts to things;
soul to senses;
eternity to time.

"God, our Father, so has M. C. given himself to you—so has he lived and will live with you. We are so grateful for this experience. In the spirit of Christ we pray. Amen."

Those who have experienced such praying in depth, using the directed affirmation method, will be first to testify as to the difference between "being prayed for" and "being prayed in."

This approach may be effectively used under many different circumstances. Mr. R. N. had an experience of total-mind faithing when in the hospital with a broken back. Though he had, under the doctor's guidance, decided to have an operation, he was afraid, not of dying (as he put it), but of the added pain which it would bring, since his present pain was all but unbearable. This is how he described the experience of praying in depth, using the directed affirmation.

"The evening before the operation was to take place, my

pastor came to see me. He talked for quite a while with me, and finally, just before it was time to turn off the lights, he asked me this question: 'Bob, do you *really* want to get well?'

" 'Sure!'

"He asked the question again, and I gave him the same answer. He then said, 'Well, then, let go and let God.'

"Let go and let God! That was a new idea for me, and I thought of it for a few minutes.

"At this point he had me get as comfortable as was possible, and had the nurse leave the room so that I could go to sleep. He then led me in a faith rehearsal of the anticipated events of the coming day and the coming week in terms of God's love. One statement I remember very clearly: 'Place your hands beneath Bob's body and completely heal it. He will have no more pain—no more pain.'

"I went to sleep that night knowing that everything was going to be all right. I awoke from that peaceful sleep only after the operation had been completed (six hours long) and had another natural sleep of twelve hours. I couldn't believe that the operation had been completed until the nurses had me feel a specially cut hole in my body cast. This hole allowed the nurses to dress the incision in my back.

"To this day I have never felt pain in connection with that operation. My pastor worked with me every day for about two weeks, teaching me how to use this faithing process; then I began to feel that I didn't want to see him anymore. I wanted to try and share this thing that he had given me with other people—and still do."

There is little that the pastor can bring to a pre-operative patient that can help him more than faithing in depth. In the course of our conversations I had well in mind the person R. N. wanted to be, and (after some time spent in physical and mental surrender) described it to him in careful detail, leading him to accept the Spirit of God as literally making him that person.

Or take the case of Mrs. E. C., who was catapulted into a family crisis when her husband became seriously ill. We will let her describe how "faithing in depth" through the use of directed affirmation helped her to give God a chance in her life (note *how* she came to feel *what* she believed).

"One beautiful summer day several years ago, my world fell apart. At ten o'clock my husband was well and happily preparing for a family outing. Twenty minutes later he was in the hospital critically ill.

"After the first unbelieving shock, I was consumed with fear; fear for his life, or if he lived, fear of his being crippled; fear of my own inadequacies—could I prepare our three children for what might lie ahead; would I ever be free of dread and panic; could I find enough faith for both of us to carry us through the hours and days ahead?

"There was only one possible source of help for me and, with the help of my pastor, I turned to prayer. Never had I needed prayer as I needed it then. Many times I was so numb, and my mind so full of dread, that it was impossible to concentrate. Sometimes I would call him to pray for me. Later I would try to use his words, and I would just assume the attitude of prayer. It was always very difficult for me to return to the hospital; I so feared what I might find when I entered that room. I found that repeating the Twenty-third Psalm over and over again gave me the strength to get there.

"One day my pastor suggested I come to his office for a private worship service. I was hesitant to go because this personal approach to God was so new to me. But my need was so great that I made an appointment.

"A deep, total-mind faithing-therapy session is a wonderful experience. At first there is a feeling of complete relaxation, a drifting away from the immediate tensions and problems. It is not a sleepy feeling, but the feeling of the presence of God. There is such a feeling of release and of being cleansed; a return or renewal of faith, and a desire to meet the problems that had previously seemed too large.

"I remember going back to the hospital after that first session, able to smile and feeling a strength for myself and hope for my husband that were depleted when I had first gone to see my pastor.

"After I was able to accept the wonder of this release, I was most concerned that I would find myself too dependent upon my pastor. Finding someone who could listen to me with understanding but without pity; someone who could direct my thinking constructively and clearly; someone who could lead me to believe in myself and the healing power of God, became so vital to me that I was concerned that I might never feel competent alone. . . .

"As the sessions went deeper, my faithing became more meaningful and the will to believe and know the love of God was stronger. My fears were more easily overcome, and I felt a child of God for greater lengths of time. This did not happen quickly, but over a period of many months and daily faithing.

"Then one day, during a directed faithing session, I had a religious experience I shall never forget. I was so surrounded by God, and he was so much a part of me. It was such a quiet feeling; such a 'knowing' that he was with me. This is what I had been hearing about from the pulpit all my life—the intangible, elusive thing I never expected to know. It now seems so simple. Of course God loves me, is all around me, and will be with me always. There is a warmth and joy in my heart I did not know before. I am sustained. I no longer pray to God, but with God.

"This is surely just the beginning, and I pray that I shall grow in the sight of God."

I should state further that after a time (the more we have pulling us down, the more difficult it is to stay up), Mrs. E. C. learned how to use the personal affirmation in her private devotions so as to attain great depths of faithing on her own.

It may be profitable for me to share more testimony, from my experience, in using the directed affirmation, but in a manner which does not take as much of the counsellor's service.

I have found the use of a tape recorder of great help to some people when they make repeated use of a directed affirmation session. Take the case of C. B., who had an unusually able mind. As you talked with him in social life, you felt a deep warmth in his personality. But C. B. had a way of piling up tensions to the place where he would literally "blow up inside." This is how he described himself and his success with faithing in depth.

"I guess that I had always been a worrywart. I had always let things upset me which shouldn't. While in graduate school, a great many little things began to pile up to worry me. First, there were the normal pressures of graduate school: tests, research, preliminary exams, speeches, and so forth; then there was the question of finding a job after I left school and the interview trips involved. There were the problems of adjusting to marriage—the normal in-law difficulties. Finally, there was a severe personality conflict with a fellow student with whom I worked closely.

"As these pressures began to pile up, I became increasingly irritable. I worried more, especially at night. Sleeping pills became a necessity for sleep. The culmination of all this was emergency surgery for hemorrhaging duodenal ulcers. Following this surgery I was told by my doctors to relax, stay calm, quit worrying, and so forth. This was good advice, but I had no idea how to follow it. Within a few months I was in critical condition in a hospital with more hemorrhaging. I was out of the hospital four days and then back again—bleeding once more.

"It was at this time that I went to my minister with my problem, which had now become a life-or-death matter. The minister worked with me through deep-faith therapy. In this therapy I came to feel God helping me attain the qualities necessary for a normal life. Key words were *calmness, confidence, peace,* and *serenity,* along with a general sense of facing problems of life with confidence and calmly solving them.

"The effect on my life was fantastic. I accepted problems and struggled with their solutions, but I didn't have any internal turmoil or worry problems. I could sleep at night and wake up to confidently face another day with its problems.

"The minister's work with me was quite intense, but for a short time only, since I was finishing graduate school and moving out of town. However, by the time I left Illinois I was at the point where I no longer needed him in person, but he still directed me in faith therapy via a tape recorder. In addition, I had learned to faith by myself. With the help of God and the techniques taught me by my pastor, I was able to establish the kind of person I wanted to be.

"I used the tape recorder for several months after moving. I still practice faithing, and find that I confidently face the world and calmly struggle with the problems thrown my way. I can't solve them all, but I calmly attack them and do not let them disturb me.

"My health (both mental and physical) has been excellent the past four years. I have had many problems to deal with—making family adjustments, with two children now in the family; serious family trouble with my brother and his wife; difficulties with in-laws; struggling in a new job; a severe personality conflict with a fellow worker; the problem of supervision over people following a promotion at work; trying to settle a neighborhood conflict. Some of these problems have been successfully solved. Others, I believe, cannot be solved. But the important fact is that, through faithing, I have been able to face all these problems with no ill effects. I actually enjoy them as a challenge. I get sincere joy from solving them, while at the same time I can easily accept a failure with the confidence and calmness that comes from feeling that I have done my best. I can gratefully say that 'faithing' has given me a new, confident, happy, more Christian outlook on life."

May I state again that those who, through the directed affirmation, are led to pray in depth will find that the experience was invaluable to them as they seek for the same experience through the personal affirmation. However, we must not assume that the value of the personal affirmation is dependent upon the directed affirmation. To the contrary, the personal affirmation stands at the very center of the devotional life of every Christian, no matter what his devotional approach may be.

Let us now turn to the personal affirmation.

The Personal Affirmation

Leslie Weatherhead has quoted a Cambridge scientist who told his class why he became a Christian.

"I was brought up in a Christian home with my brother, and the two of us were the closest pals. We were both at the university together. My father and mother were deeply religious. My brother and I had no time for religion. We thought that religion was all right for old people, but we were scientists and we thought we had found our way through by what we were pleased to call scientific methods. Then my brother was killed. My father and mother had resources, and with their resources they could meet that shattering loss. But I had no one. I had no resources at all. One night, broken-hearted and with all my proud science in ruined uselessness at my feet, I knelt down. I did not know how to pray. I had scorned prayer, but I put out my hand"— and then, in deep emotion, the lecturer went on—"and *I found it was grasped.* I knew that someone was coming to my help and, somehow, I knew it was Christ. I have been a Christian ever since and no one, nothing, will take Christ from me any more." (1)

As we have stated above, it is not uncommon for men to mature in their feeling relationship to God and to life during times of crises. We would like to point the way to attain this God-sense for everyday living. I question if Jesus was any more God-conscious at Gethsemane than when he was among his friends at Bethany or when fishing. Others may have been as God-aware as was he for short periods, but Jesus was deeply aware of God most of the time. Jesus' faith was a faith "for the living of these days."

As we proceed, let us keep firmly in mind our definition of a Christian: one who relates in Jesus' way to God, self, others, and conditions about him. The question is, How does one use the personal affirmation to assist himself, or others, in making these relationships in Jesus' way? How does one get this "power to become" for himself or others? To answer this question, I am presenting four examples of making the faith approach to living— through the use of personal affirmations. They are in skeleton form. It is apparent, I am sure, that faithing for others (intercessory prayer) is little different from faithing for ourselves—the examples may be used in both ways.

Ways of using the personal affirmation when making:

1. The faith approach to God-directed living.

2. The faith approach to moral living.

3. The faith approach to brotherhood.

4. The faith approach to Bible reading.

These presentations hardly touch the fringes of the life situations that call for faith as over against fear-centered living. It is hoped, however, that they are different and varied enough to make quite clear the personal affirmation procedure for general use.

In each example you will note that the "where, what, who, and how" are worked out, but only as examples. Each of us must fill one out for himself. (See charts beginning on page 176.)

The Faith Approach to Private Worship through Bible Reading

Step I

Where? Begin anticipating your day and asking, "Where do I want to work more closely with God this day?" Verbalize it carefully and clearly, perhaps writing it out.

Step II

Omit in this situation.

Step III

Creating the belief self-image. Now, following whatever method you are using for selecting your reading place in the Bible, read slowly and imaginatively. Take time to pursue any hint or insight until you are seized by the "insight for the day." Examine it thoroughly in the light of your decision in Step I.

Step IV

Creating the faith self-image. Sit back, close your eyes, and prayerfully imagine yourself in the situation set forth in Step I. Sense God in your life—making you the kind of person you feel he wants you to be. Let the "insight of the day," as it were, embrace all your actions.

A Sample Worksheet for Spiritual Growth in Receiving God's Guidance in Decision Making for Self or Others

STEP I

WHERE	BELIEFS	

Decision One

Where, specifically, do you choose to improve your relating to God, Self, Others, or Conditions?

I want God's guidance in making a decision about _____

Religious		General	
1—God	XX	Ability—13	☐
2—Jesus	XX	Education—14	☐
3—Bible	☐	Position—15	☐
4—Holy Spirit	X	Appearance—16	☐
5—Prayer	☐	Handicap—17	☐
6—Faith	☐	Money—18	☐
7—Immortality	☐	Clothes—19	☐
8—Man	☐	Experience—20	☐
9—Church	☐	failure—a	Ø
10—Evil	☐	success—b	Ø
11—Intuitive awareness	X	Health—21	☐
12—Charms	☐	Personality—22	☐
		Family—23	Ø
		Example—24	Ø

Because of my belief about "X" and "O"

I believe that in my relationship

to (WHERE—Step I)

I can be (WHO—Step III-A)

YOUR BELIEF SELF-IMAGE

176

	Decision Two WHAT		Decision Three WHO	
	STEP II		STEP III	
	What is your present Feeling Self-Image in your selected improvement area?		Who do you want to be in your chosen improvement area? (Your new B.S.I.)	
	A DESCRIPTIVE WORDS— NEGATIVE	**B** Why do you think you feel as you do in this area?	**A** DESCRIPTIVE WORDS— POSITIVE	**B** Reasons for believing it is possible for you to relate this way
			Guided	*God directs all who will be directed.*
			Possessed	*He did direct Jesus' thinking*
			One	*Others have been guided*
			Surrendered	
			Have felt guided myself in the past.	

STEP IV

CREATING YOUR FAITH SELF-IMAGE

Changing knowledge into feeling—beliefs into faith. Proverbs 23:7

DECISION IN REVIEW

1. Where did you decide to be more Christian? (Step I—write in B below.)

2. What words best describe the kind of person you chose to be in your improvement area? (Step III-A—write in A below.)

3. Which beliefs (1-24) undergird your new Belief Self-Image?

4. How do you expect to practice your new B.S.I. (actually and imaginatively)?

BRINGING YOUR DECISIONS INTO PRACTICE

1. PREPARATION

A. Physically

Attain a comfortable position, either sitting or reclining. Relaxation is very desirable. Portions of the services on pages 188, 189 should be helpful.

B. Mentally—be still and receive.

Think of yourself as being as still and as quiet as light. Remember that God has something great for you, and that all you have to do is to accept it. Affirm God's power (Holy Spirit, Grace, Presence) as permeating your whole being. Think on these things: Luke 7:7, 24: 49; Phil. 2:3; John 1:2; Acts 2:15; Eph. 2:7, 8.

178

2. GOD-CENTERED IMAGINATIVE PRACTICE (including what you expect to do actually)

   A. Accept God's power as filling your total mind (conscious and subconscious).

   B. Affirm the creative power of God in your total mind as making you:

THIS KIND OF PERSON

A	Guided
	One with
	Surrendered
	Possessed

WHEN IN THIS SITUATION

B	When making a
	decision
	about ———

Affirm each descriptive word (A) one at a time, several times in the situation (B). Seek to identify with the person that you have chosen to be.

The closing prayer may be thus: "God, our Father, I accept your spirit in my total mind as making me the person I have chosen to be. As I have practiced and lived in my mind, so I am going to live with my hands, feet, and lips. I know that as you were in Jesus, so you are in me. In His spirit I pray. Amen."

3. GOD-CENTERED ACTUAL PRACTICE

   Making and taking every opportunity to be a doer of the Word. As much as possible, to do actually what you have done imaginatively and to affirm God in your life as you do it.

A Sample Worksheet for Spiritual Growth in Moral Living in Helping Self or Others

STEP I   Decision One   WHERE

Where, specifically, do you choose to improve your relating to God, Self, Others, or Conditions?

I want to be moral in my relationship to the other per in thought and act.

BELIEFS

Religious	General
1—God ☒	Ability—13 ☐
2—Jesus ☒	Education—14 ☐
3—Bible ☐	Position—15 ☐
4—Holy Spirit ☒	Appearance—16 ☐
5—Prayer ☐	Handicap—17 ☐
6—Faith ☐	Money—18 ☐
7—Immortality ☐	Clothes—19 ☐
8—Man ☐	Experience—20 ☐
9—Church ☐	failure—a ☐
10—Evil ☐	success—b ☒
11—Intuitive awareness ☐	Health—21 ☐
12—Charms ☐	Personality—22 ☐
	Family—23 ☐
	Example—24 ☒

Because of my belief about "X" and "O"

I believe that in my relationship

to (WHERE—Step I)

I can be (WHO—Step III-A)

YOUR BELIEF SELF-IMAGE

180

STEP II		Decision Two WHAT	STEP III		Decision Three WHO
What is your present Feeling Self-Image in your selected improvement area?			Who do you want to be in your chosen improvement area? (Your new B.S.I.)		
A DESCRIPTIVE WORDS— NEGATIVE		**B** Why do you think you feel as you do in this area?	**A** DESCRIPTIVE WORDS— POSITIVE		**B** Reasons for believing it is possible for you to relate this way
Lusty		Sex drive	Understanding		My belief in
Selfish		Past experience	Friendly		Jesus' way.
Guilty		Associations	Natural		Like to feel
Sneaky		Mental Practice	Generous		wholesome
					Believe in Gods
					help.
			Practice "Golden Rule"		
			Past training		

181

A Sample Worksheet for Spiritual Growth in Brotherhood for Helping Self or Others

STEP IV

CREATING YOUR FAITH SELF-IMAGE

HOW

Changing knowledge into feeling—beliefs into faith. Proverbs 23:7

DECISION IN REVIEW

1. Where did you decide to be more Christian? (Step I—write in **B** below.)

2. What words best describe the kind of person you chose to be in your improvement area? (Step III-A—write in **A** below.)

3. Which beliefs (1-24) undergird your new Belief Self-Image?

4. How do you expect to practice your new B.S.I. (actually and imaginatively)?

BRINGING YOUR DECISIONS INTO PRACTICE

1. PREPARATION

A. Physically

Attain a comfortable position, either sitting or reclining. Relaxation is very desirable. Portions of the services on pages 188, 189 should be helpful.

B. Mentally—be still and receive.

Think of yourself as being as still and as quiet as light. Remember that God has something great for you, and that all you have to do is to accept it. Affirm God's power (Holy Spirit, Grace, Presence) as permeating your whole being. Think on these things: Luke 7:7, 24: 49; Phil. 2:3; John 1:2; Acts 2:15; Eph. 2:7, 8.

2. GOD-CENTERED IMAGINATIVE PRACTICE (including what you expect to do actually)

A. Accept God's power as filling your total mind (conscious and subconscious).

B. Affirm the creative power of God in your total mind as making you:

THIS KIND OF PERSON ➡   WHEN IN THIS SITUATION ➡

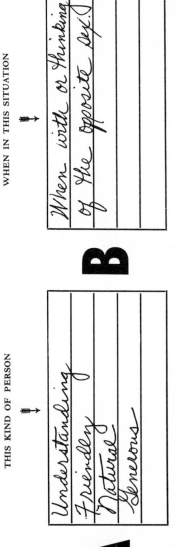

A	
Understanding	
Friendly	
Natural	
Generous	

B	
When with or thinking	
of the opposite sex.)	

Affirm each descriptive word (A) one at a time, several times in the situation (B). Seek to identify with the person that you have chosen to be. The closing prayer may be thus: "God, our Father, I accept your spirit in my total mind as making me the person I have chosen to be. As I have practiced and lived in my mind, so I am going to live with my hands, feet, and lips. I know that as you were in Jesus, so you are in me. In His spirit I pray. Amen."

3. GOD-CENTERED ACTUAL PRACTICE

Making and taking every opportunity to be a doer of the Word. As much as possible, to do actually what you have done imaginatively and to affirm God in your life as you do it.

183

STEP I Decision One WHERE   BELIEFS General

Where, specifically, do you choose to improve your relating to God, Self, Others, or Conditions?

With other races

Religious		General	
1—God	⊠	Ability—13	☐
2—Jesus	⊠	Education—14	☐
3—Bible	⊠	Position—15	☐
4—Holy Spirit	⊠	Appearance—16	☐
5—Prayer	⊠	Handicap—17	☐
6—Faith	⊠	Money—18	☐
7—Immortality	☐	Clothes—19	☐
8—Man	☐	Experience—20	☐
9—Church	☐	failure—a	☐
10—Evil	☐	success—b	☐
11—Intuitive		Health—21	☐
awareness	☐	Personality—22	☐
12—Charms	☐	Family—23	☐
		Example—24	⌀

Because of my belief about "X" and "O"

I believe that in my relationship

to (WHERE—Step I)

I can be (WHO—Step III-A)

YOUR BELIEF SELF-IMAGE

184

Decision Two		Decision Three		WHO
STEP II	WHAT	STEP III		
What is your present Feeling Self-Image in your selected improvement area?		Who do you want to be in your chosen improvement area? (Your new B.S.I.)		

A — DESCRIPTIVE WORDS—NEGATIVE	B — Why do you think you feel as you do in this area?	A — DESCRIPTIVE WORDS—POSITIVE	B — Reasons for believing it is possible for you to relate this way
Conscious	Past conditioning by associates and family.	Brotherly	All men God's children. I know those of other races more Christ-like than I.
Repelled		Friendly	
Superior		Equal	
Resentful		Secure	
		Jesus taught brotherhood. The power of faith and prayer.	

185

CREATING YOUR FAITH SELF-IMAGE

Changing knowledge into feeling—beliefs into faith. Proverbs 23:7

DECISION IN REVIEW

1. Where did you decide to be more Christian? (Step I—write in B below.)

2. What words best describe the kind of person you chose to be in your improvement area? (Step III-A—write in A below.)

3. Which beliefs (1-24) undergird your new Belief Self-Image?

4. How do you expect to practice your new B.S.I. (actually and imaginatively)?

BRINGING YOUR DECISIONS INTO PRACTICE

1. PREPARATION

   A. Physically

   Attain a comfortable position, either sitting or reclining. Relaxation is very desirable. Portions of the services on pages 188, 189 should be helpful.

   B. Mentally—be still and receive.

   Think of yourself as being, as still and as quiet as light. Remember that God has something great for you, and that all you have to do is to accept it. Affirm God's power (Holy Spirit, Grace, Presence) as permeating your whole being. Think on these things: Luke 7:7, 24: 49; Phil. 2:3; John 1:2; Acts 2:15; Eph. 2:7, 8.

2. GOD-CENTERED IMAGINATIVE PRACTICE (including what you expect to do actually)

  A. Accept God's power as filling your total mind (conscious and subconscious).

  B. Affirm the creative power of God in your total mind as making you:

THIS KIND OF PERSON ➤   WHEN IN THIS SITUATION ➤

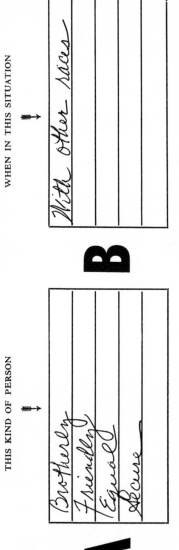

A

Brotherly
Friendly
Equal
Secure

B

With Other Races

Affirm each descriptive word (A) one at a time, several times in the situation (B). Seek to identify with the person that you have chosen to be.

The closing prayer may be thus: "God, our Father, I accept your spirit in my total mind as making me the person I have chosen to be. As I have practiced and lived in my mind, so I am going to live with my hands, feet, and lips. I know that as you were in Jesus, so you are in me. In His spirit I pray. Amen."

3. GOD-CENTERED ACTUAL PRACTICE

  Making and taking every opportunity to be a doer of the Word. As much as possible, to do actually what you have done imaginatively and to affirm God in your life as you do it.

A Spiritual-Affirmation Approach
to Private Worship

Here you have an affirmative statement of some choice scripture verses. The first service (page 189) should always be used; then this should be followed with any of the other services for which you may feel a special need. We would suggest the following procedure:

1. Read a line (while lying or sitting); close your eyes and absorb the meaning of the affirmation. (You may want to look up the scripture reference; commit it to memory and repeat it in the atmosphere of the affirmation.)
2. When your mind begins to wander, open your eyes and read the next affirmation. As above, again close your eyes and absorb the meaning of the affirmation. During the meditation period, between affirmations, mentally repeat such thoughts from the former affirmations as cling to your memory.
3. Take your time. Be unhurried.
4. This worship procedure will prove especially helpful before going to sleep at night, and particularly so when it has been memorized.

SURRENDER TO WORSHIP

Let Us Pray

Prayer is the *soul's sincere desire,*
Unuttered or expressed;
The *motion* of a *hidden fire*
That *trembles* in the *breast.*

O Thou, by whom *we come to God,*
The *Life,* the *Truth,* the *Way;*
The path of *prayer Thyself* hast trod;
Lord, teach *us how* to *pray.*

Thou art a Spirit and I worship Thee in spirit and in truth.	
	JOHN 4:24
Bathed in stillness, I know that Thou art God.	PSALM 46:10
I seek first Thy Kingdom.	MATT. 6:33
Into Thy hands I commit my spirit.	PSALM 31:5
I accept as good Thy will for me.	1 TIM. 4:4
Whatsoever things are true, honest, just, pure, lovely. . . .	
I think on these.	PHIL. 4:8
I surrender my life to faith.	MATT. 9:29
In Thy Spirit I find all worth and meaning.	ROM. 9:7-8
I yield to Thee with my whole heart.	JER. 29:13
My mind is set on things above.	COL. 3:2
I join with Thee in creative love.	JOHN 1:3
In Thee, I see all things clearly.	1 JOHN 1:5

A QUIET MIND IN A RELAXED BODY

I surrender my body to rest. I am relaxed in Thee.	
As I yield, Thou dost possess.	1 COR. 3:23
Thou dost feed my soul in quietness.	PSALM 127:2
In peace I lay me down to sleep.	PSALM 4:8
The peace of God, which passeth all understanding, guards	
my heart and thoughts in Christ Jesus.	PHIL. 4:7

Thou dost make all storms a calm.	PSALM 107:29
Into Thy quietness there can no trouble come.	JOB 34:29
I live in peace.	2 COR. 13:11
All my experiences come together and lie down in peace.	ISA. 11:6-9
I am in nothing anxious.	PHIL. 4:6
Thou dost keep me in perfect peace. My mind is stayed on Thee.	ISA. 26:3
In the stillness of my own heart I commune with Thee in peace.	PSALM 4:4
Not as the world giveth, givest Thou unto me.	JOHN 14:27
Thy yoke is easy.	MATT. 11:30
Sweet is Thy rest.	PROV. 3:24
I am Thine. I rest in loving trust.	ISA. 32:17-18
I wait upon Thee. I renew my strength.	ISA. 40:31

THE PRACTICE OF GOD'S NEARNESS

In Thine image I am made.	GEN. 2:27
In Thee I find life.	JOB 33:4
Thou hast made all things—Thou art God.	HEB. 3:4
I live in love. I dwell in Thee.	1 JOHN 4:16
I am with Thee, and all is good.	PSALM 33:5
In Thee I live and move and have my being	ACTS 17:28
I find my beginning and my eternity in Thee.	REV. 1:8
My sufficiency is in Thee, O God.	2 COR. 3:5
Thy Spirit doth hold my spirit on high.	PSALM 139:9-10
Thy word is a lamp unto my feet.	PSALM 119:105
In Thee I am made free from all entangling places.	PSALM 25:15
Thou dost reveal all things unto me by Thy Spirit.	1 COR. 2:10

How excellent is Thy loving kindness, O God. PSALM 36:7

I bless Thee for Thy goodness to all men. PSALM 107:8

I love Thee with all my heart, soul, and mind. MATT. 22:37

Thou art with me always, even to the end. MATT. 28:20

Thou art my shepherd, I shall not want. PSALM 23

I will fear no evil; for Thou art with me. PSALM 23

I will dwell in Thy presence forever and ever. PSALM 23

THE PRACTICE OF CONFIDENCE AND MENTAL HEALTH

Father God, I turn to Thee in confidence.

Thou dost keep me in perfect peace; my mind is stayed
on Thee. ISA. 26:3

I have no fear of what I cannot see. PSALM 91:5

I know Thy truth. I am free to be myself. JOHN 8:32

I let that mind be in me which was also in Christ Jesus. PHIL. 2:5

In Christ's strength I find strength. PHIL. 4:13

In Thy light I see light. PSALM 36:9

I renew my mind in Christ Jesus. ROM. 12:2

I forsake the ways and the thoughts of evil. ISA. 55:7

I follow Jesus in all things. JOHN 14:12

Thou hast made me to have dominion. PSALM 8:6-8

I let Thy love realize its strength in me. PHIL. 3:13

Thy Kingdom is power. 1 COR. 4:20

I seek first Thy Kingdom and let all things be added
unto me. MATT. 6:33

I lose myself in Thy loving abundance. 1 COR. 2:9

In Thee I find freedom to be myself. 2 COR. 3:17

Perfect love in me casteth out all fear. 1 JOHN 4:18

Thou art with me—I am beyond all fear.	ISA. 43:5
Loving Thee, all things work together for good.	ROM. 8:28
I am swallowed up in victory.	JOHN 16:33
My heart is fixed, trusting in Thee.	PSALM 112:7
In Thee there is no failing.	2 CHRON. 20:17
I do believe. I do receive.	MARK 11:24
I accept Thy abundance in faith, nothing doubting.	JAMES 1:5-7
In Thine image, I am created constantly.	GEN. 1:27
As I am pure, all things are pure.	TITUS 1:15
Goodness and mercy follow me everywhere.	PSALM 23:6
With Thee I find all strength; I am confident.	PSALM 27:1
Forgiving all, I am forgiven.	LUKE 6:37
Confident of Thy forgiving love, I start anew.	JER. 33:8
	PSALM 32:11
	REV. 21:5
	ISA. 1:18
	ISA. 6:7
	PSALM 86:5
	HEBREWS 10:17
In Christ I am a new creature.	2 COR. 5:17

THE PRACTICE OF FAITH IN SEARCH OF HEALTH

The word of healing doth abound in me.	PSALM 107:20
In Thee I find happiness through strength.	NEH. 8:10
As are my days, so is my strength.	DEUT. 33:25
Thou doth glorify Thyself in my flesh.	1 COR. 6:20
Healing of body; cheerfulness of heart, art mine in Thee.	PROV. 17:22
Faith hath made me whole.	MARK 10:52

Thou doth put Thy spirit in me. It healeth my
infirmities.   Rom. 8:26
    Ezek. 37:14

With long life doth Thou satisfy me.   Psalm 91:16

Thy word hath taken command in my life; I am healed.
Behold, Thou doth make all things new.   Rev. 21:5

Thou doth heal all my diseases; my youth is renewed
like the eagles.   Psalm 103:3-5

Thou art the God of all flesh. All things are possible
in Thee.   Jer. 32:27

I yield, that Thou mayest perfect that which concerneth
my prayer.   Psalm 138:8

Thy word is truth; Thy word is power.   Luke 1:37

Thou doth know the life in every living thing.   Job 12:10

Thy healing spirit worketh in me.   Ex. 15:26

In Thy presence I feel strength.   Jer. 30:11

In Thee even my weakness is made into strength.   2 Cor. 12:9

Faith hath saved me: I go in peace.   Luke 7:50

I ask, and Thou dost give; now I give as Thou
dost ask.   Psalm 21:2-4

My spirit gathereth strength with friends in prayer; we feel
Thy presence.   Matt. 18:19-20; Psalm 145:15-16

My prayer is effectual, for it is fervent.   James 5:16

With quiet confidence I enter into the blessings of
prayer.   John 11:22

My body is Thy temple; Thou dost dwell there.   1 Cor. 3:16

I arise to go forth in Thy name.   Matt. 9:6-7

In returning to Thee, I return to the best in me.   Job 22:23

It is in seeking Thee that I satisfy my wants.
    Psalm 37:4; Psalm 34:10

The Practice of Immortality

I know that Thou hast made me like Thyself.   GEN. 1:27

I have eternity in me. I am joint heir with Christ.   TITUS 3:6

I rest in Thee. I wait in patience.   PSALM 37:7

I sit at the feet of my eternity and listen.   JOHN 14:2-4

I cast all anxiety aside. Thou dost care for me.   I PETER 5:7

I believe in Thee. I yield.   HEBREWS 11:6

I feel Thy Kingdom in me.   MATT. 6:10

Though I am weak, yet am I strong.   2 COR. 12:10

Thou dost stand by.   2 TIM. 4:17

To know Thee is to be free from all iniquity.   JOHN 8:11

There is no separating me from Christ.   ROM. 8:38-39

I am blessed in Thee with the fruits of faith.   JER. 17:7-8

I cast my all upon Thee; Thou dost sustain me.   PSALM 55:22

Thou that revealeth life eternal giveth it to me.   ROM. 8:11

The freedom of eternity is mine now. I am immortal
    now.   PHIL. 3:21

In the gifts of the spirit doth my soul prosper.   JOHN 6:63

Death is powerless in me.   HOS. 13:14

Forgetting the things which are behind and
    stretching forward to the things which
    are before, I press on toward the goal
    unto the prize of the high calling of
    God in Christ Jesus.   PHIL. 3:13-14

The Creative Practice of Brotherhood

Thou art Father of us all.   MAL. 2:10

Thou hast made of one blood all nations of men.
                    ACTS 17:26; MATT. 19:19

I live at peace with all men.	ROM. 12:18
I forgive all as Thou hast forgiven me.	EPH. 4:32
I owe no man anything but to love him.	ROM. 13:8
No man can take from me as much as I will give.	MATT. 5:39-41
Bearing another's burdens, I thereby fulfill the love of Christ.	GAL. 6:2
As I love all men, I know I am Thine.	JOHN 13:35
Love is of Thee, O God. I love all men.	1 JOHN 4:7-8
All that I do is done in love.	1 COR. 16:14
I love all men with a pure heart.	1 JOHN 3:11 1 PETER 1:22
My mind is pure toward my neighbor.	ZECH. 8:17 PSALM 66:18 MARK 11:25
To all that ask, I give. I turn not away.	MARK 9:41 MATT. 5:42
To help and serve all men is my first desire.	PROV. 25:21-22
In Christ I am all things to all men.	ROM. 12:15 1 COR. 9:22
I love Thee in deed and in truth.	1 JOHN 3:18
I let my light so shine before men that they may see my good works and fulfill Thy love in my heart.	MATT. 5:16 1 JOHN 4:12
I so live that all men may live in peace.	MATT. 5:9
I turn to all men with loving kindness.	JAMES 4:11 JAMES 1:26
I look not just to my own, but to the good of all.	PHIL. 2:3-4
Out of my strength I bear the infirmities of the weak.	ROM. 15:1-2
In my heart all men live together in cooperative fellowship.	ISA. 41:6-7

My good returneth unto me in abundance.　　　　Luke 6:38

Releasing all, I am released.　　　　Luke 6:37

I judge no man, but help all to live.　　　　Rom. 14:13
　　　　Gal. 6:1

I overcome all evil with good.　　　　1 Thess. 5:14-15

A Comprehensive Biblical Affirmation Service of Worship

　　　Prayer is the soul's sincere desire,
　　　Unuttered or expressed;
　　　The motion of a hidden fire
　　　That trembles in the breast.

　　　O Thou, by whom we come to God,
　　　The Life, the Truth, the Way;
　　　The path of prayer Thyself hast trod;
　　　Lord, teach us how to pray.

O Thou, Great Spirit, help me now to pray.
Pray Thou in me.
Make me Thy prayer.
As Thou art, so help me be.
All that I have is Thine.
I am unhurried.
My body, my nerves, my self—all are Thine.
My arms and legs are limp with abandonment.
In Thee I am relaxed, all relaxed.
I rest in complete peace.
Prayerfully, I am free from strain.
Free from all strain, I am relaxed.
Every nerve of my body is faith-filled.
All tension has gone from my body.
I am quiet, all quiet, way down on the inside.
I am alone with God, lost in His spirit.
Bathed in His peace.
I and Christos are one.
I accept the mind of Christ.

I am free from all fear.
I am filled with faith.
My soul is at peace in Thee.
My arms and legs are limp with abandonment.
I am relaxed.
Completely relaxed.
In the name of Jesus I am above all worry.
All troubles fall free from my spirit.
I dismiss all worry from my mind.
I am filled with faith power.
I am at peace.
I want nothing for myself.
I am free to be myself.
I am faith-filled.
Love-filled.
Christ-filled.
I am a new person in God's love.
I accept the mind of Christ.
I am poised.
With all people.
In all places.
I am at all times at prayer.
Poised in prayer.
I let that poise be in me which was also in Christ Jesus.
In confidence I accept the mind of Christ.
I am confident.
With all people.
In all places.
My mind is clothed in peace.
I and Christ are one.
The peace of God is mine.
I am in His peace relaxed.

IN BRIEF

We have proposed that all Christian religions have one
thing in common: a feeling that is the opposite of fear, which,
for lack of a better name, we call "faith."

Faith we have found to be beliefs emotionalized. We do not have faith until we have the substance of the hope—not just the hope.

The establishing of these hopes (beliefs), we observed, is the intellectual side of religion, whereas the feeling (faith) side comes from experience, both actual and imaginative.

We also have perceived that there are three basic ways to stimulate faith-creating imaginative experience—diversion, reason, and suggestion. Under "suggestion" we placed special emphasis on the use of the directed and personal affirmation.

My only hope is that this will mean as much to you as it has meant to me and the many with whom I have worked and shared through the years.

Appendix

FORMING A GROUP

Developing a Group

1. Discuss some of the phases of the material with some friends, and see if they seem interested.
2. Tell them that you would like to discuss it with them in more detail, and that you would be glad to loan them your book.
3. When you get a recruit, solicit his help in finding other interested people.

   Remember, six couples (or twelve persons) is a large enough group.

Using an Established Group

1. An adult class
   A. After a presentation, divide into small groups for discussion.
2. A social group (Let them select the leader.)
   A. Take a forty-five-minute period for discussion.

CONDUCTING A STUDY GROUP

Using This or Other Books

1. At the first session
   A. Have someone prepared to present the book as a whole and state why the book is of interest to the group.
   B. Decide on procedure for next meeting—when and where.
      a. You may find it helpful to assign yourself definite pages for study.

b. Divide the selected pages into four to six units and assign them to as many people.
(Some groups have their social and refreshment time first and close with the discussion and faithing service. Others like to have the discussion first. Meeting in different homes, with two families serving as "hosts," has been found practical.)

2. Format for second and following sessions
   A. Pause for a moment of silent prayer.
   B. The one having the first unit will give a summary of the position set forth in the book—as they see it.
   C. After each summary, the group should test it for accuracy. "Do you all read the unit with the same understanding?"
   D. Discuss the position taken in the book and any footnote questions.

The Worship Service at the Close

1. The faithing time must have a leader.
2. Have some prayer projects (not too many).
3. Decide who or what you want to faith and what you want to accomplish (one of your group may be the object of your faithing); then
   A. Follow the formats (pages 175 to 182), using the intercessory approach
   or
   B. Use the comprehensive worship service—pages 188-89
   or
   C. Bible reading; following the format—page 175
   or
   D. Work up your own approach.
4. Always plan your faithing follow-up with as much actual experience as possible.
5. Discuss your personal use of faithing in your private devotions—to the end of helping each other.

Bibliography

CHAPTER I

1. Paul Tillich, *Systematic Theology*, Vol. II (Chicago: University of Chicago Press, 1957). Page 107.
2. Dr. Harold Bosley, Christ Church Methodist, Park Avenue at 60th Street, N. W., New York. Used in a sermon.
3. Tracey K. Jones, Jr., *Our Mission Today* (New York: World Outlook Press, 1963). Page 72.
4. *Ibid.* Page 72. Quoting from Nicholas Berdyaev, *The Destiny of Man* (New York: Harper & Row, Publishers, Inc., 1937). Pages 146-147.
5. *Ibid.* Page 39. See Hendrik Kraemer, *World Culture and World Religions: The Coming Dialogue* (Philadelphia: The Westminster Press, 1960). Page 12.

CHAPTER II

1. Carroll A. Wise, *Psychiatry and the Bible* (New York: Harper & Brothers, 1956). Pages 2-3.
2. Karl Menninger, *Theory of Psychoanalytic Technique* (New York: Science Editions, 1961). Page 164.
3. *Ibid.* Page 178.
4. Elton Trueblood, *The Company of the Committed* (New York: Harper & Brothers, 1961). Page 23.
5. Hazen G. Werner, *No Saints Suddenly* (Nashville: Abingdon Press, 1963). Page 54.
6. Robert C. Leslie, *Jesus and Logotherapy* (Nashville: Abingdon Press, 1965). Pages 34-35.
7. M. Arthur Kline, "Psychiatrist Discovers God: We are Born to Believe," *Woman's Home Companion*, April, 1954. Page 4.
8. Robert C. Leslie, *op. cit.* Page 63.

9. Hazen G. Werner, *op. cit.* Page 116.
10. Paul Tournier, *The Healing of Persons* (New York: Harper & Row, Publishers, Inc., 1965). Page 167.
11. Robert C. Leslie, *op. cit.* Pages 28-29.
12. Anonymous, "My Fair-Weather Faith," *Redbook Magazine*, February, 1965.
13. Hazen G. Werner, *op. cit.* Page 116.
14. Robert C. Leslie, *op. cit.* Page 51.
15. Hazen G. Werner, *op. cit.* Page 52.

Chapter III

1. George W. Cornell, *The Wind and Its Ways* (New York: Association Press, 1963). Pages 15-16.
2. William T. Watkins, *The Nature and Meaning of Christian Faith* (Nashville: Tidings, 1960). Page 13.
3. William Hordern, *The Case for a New Reformation Theology* (Philadelphia: The Westminster Press, 1959). Page 72.
4. Herbert Spencer, *Social Statistics* (New York: Robert Schalkenbach Foundation, 1954). Pages 382, 384, 385.
5. Bishop F. Gerald Ensley in an address given at Marsh Chapel, Boston University, Sept. 19, 1963.
6. Harry Emerson Fosdick, *Riverside Sermons* (New York: Harper and Brothers, 1958). Page 99.
7. Herbert Butterfield in the Introduction to Arthur Koestler, *The Sleepwalkers* (New York: The Macmillan Company, 1959). Page 15.
8. Arthur Koestler, *The Sleepwalkers* (New York: The Macmillan Company, 1959). Page 199.
9. J. Wesley Robb, *An Inquiry into Faith* (Nashville: National Methodist Student Movement, 1960). Page 58.

Chapter IV

1. C. H. Dodd, *The Bible Today* (New York: Cambridge University Press, 1947). Page 92.
2. Paul Tillich, *The New Being* (New York: Charles Scribner's Sons, 1955). Page 43.

CHAPTER V

1. William T. Watkins, *The Nature and Meaning of Christian Faith* (Nashville: Tidings, 1960). Page 59.
2. Hazen G. Werner, *No Saints Suddenly* (Nashville: Abingdon Press, 1963). Page 80.
3. C. F. Von Weizsacker, *The History of Nature* (The University of Chicago Press, 1959).
4. J. Wesley Robb, *An Inquiry into Faith* (Nashville: National Methodist Student Movement, 1960). Page 32.
5. Frederick A. Norwood, *Great Moments in Church History* (Nashville: The Graded Press, 1962). Page 32.
6. *Ibid.* Pages 76-77.
7. Buel Trowbridge, *Religion for Our Times* (Washington, D.C.: Public Affairs Press, 1963). Pages 5-6.
8. L. Harold DeWolf, *The Case for Theology in the Liberal Perspective* (Philadelphia: The Westminster Press, 1959). Page 24.
9. Buel Trowbridge, *op. cit.* Page 112.

CHAPTER VI

1. Harry Emerson Fosdick, *Dear Mr. Brown* (New York: Harper & Brothers, 1961). Page 37.
2. Loudon Wainwright, "The View from Here," *Life Magazine,* Aug. 6, 1965. Page 14.
3. George Orwell, *1984* (New York: Harcourt Brace & Co., 1949). Page 36.
4. Frederick A. Norwood, *Great Moments in Church History* (Nashville: The Graded Press, 1962). Page 84.

CHAPTER VII

1. Hazen G. Werner, *No Saints Suddenly* (Nashville: Abingdon Press, 1963). Page 98.
2. Maxwell Maltz, *Psychocybernetics* (Englewood Cliffs, N.J.: Prentice-Hall, Inc., 1960). Preface.
3. *Family Week,* June 25, 1961.

CHAPTER VIII

1. Alfred Adler, *Understanding Human Nature* (Garden City, N.Y.: Garden City Publishing Co., Inc. 1927). Pages 22-23.
2. F. Gerald Ensley, *Persons Can Change* (Nashville: Graded Press, 1963). Page 96.
3. Charles Stevenson, "Heroes Who Come Home," *The Rotarian,* July 1944.
4. Karl Menninger, *Theory of Psychoanalytic Technique* (New York: Science Editions, 1961). Pages 91-94.
5. Thomas R. Kelly, *A Testament of Devotion* (New York: Harper & Brothers, 1941). Page 43.
6. Harry Emerson Fosdick, *Riverside Sermons* (New York: Harper & Brothers, 1958). Page 115.
7. Roy L. Smith, "Faith Works That Way," *The Christian Advocate,* Feb. 11, 1943.
8. E. Stanley Jones, *Abundant Living* (New York, Nashville: Abingdon-Cokesbury Press, 1942). Page 158.
9. Max Beerbohm, *The Happy Hypocrite, a Fairy Tale for Tired Men* (New York: John Lane Company, 1897).
10. Alson J. Smith, *Faith to Live by* (Garden City, N.Y.: Doubleday & Co., Inc. 1949). Pages 218-220.

CHAPTER IX

1. Robert C. Leslie, *Jesus and Logotherapy* (Nashville: Abingdon Press, 1965). Pages 22-23.
2. Gerald Kennedy, *A Reader's Notebook* (New York: Harper & Brothers, 1953). Page 93.
3. William Glasser, M.D., *Reality Therapy, A New Approach to Psychology* (New York, Evanston, London: Harper & Row, 1965). Pages 9-12, 13.
4. *Ibid.* Pages 94-96.

CHAPTER X

1. Hazen G. Werner, *No Saints Suddenly* (Nashville: Abingdon Press, 1963). Page 45. See Leslie D. Weatherhead, *Key Next Door* (Nashville: Abingdon Press, 1960). Page 140.